The Wreck
of the
Whaleship *Essex*

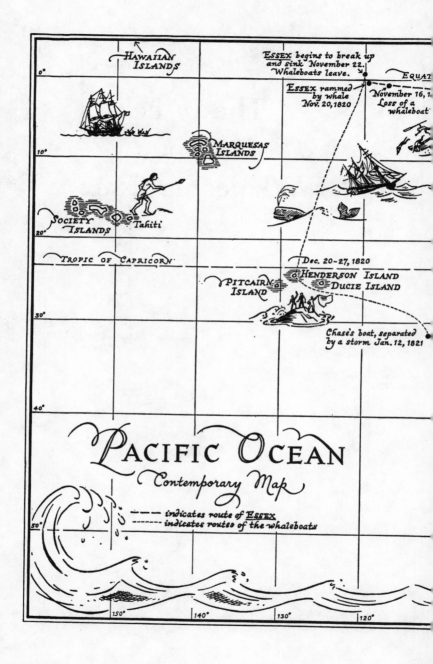

HAWAIIAN
ISLANDS

0°

ESSEX begins to break up
and sink November 22.
Whaleboats leave.

EQUA⟨T⟩

ESSEX rammed
by whale
Nov. 20, 1820

November 16, 1,
Loss of a
whaleboat

MARQUESAS
ISLANDS

10°

SOCIETY
ISLANDS   Tahiti

20°

TROPIC OF CAPRICORN

Dec. 20-27, 1820

HENDERSON ISLAND
DUCIE ISLAND

PITCAIRN
ISLAND

30°

Chase's boat, separated
by a storm Jan. 12, 1821

40°

PACIFIC OCEAN

Contemporary Map

- - - - indicates route of ESSEX
- - - - - indicates routes of the whaleboats

50°

150°   140°   130°   120°

GALÁPAGOS ISLANDS

BOGOTÁ
COLOMBIA

ESSEX sails
westward Oct.23.
after procuring
360 turtles

HOOD
ISLAND

QUITO
EQUADOR

BRAZIL

CHARLES ISLAND

ESSEX leaves
South American
coast Oct.2,1820

P
E
R
U

10°

LIMA

BOLIVIA

20°

Cruising
for whales

C
H
I
L
E

A
R
G
E
N
T
I
N
A

30°

ASTER
SLAND

Chase and two seamen
rescued Feb.18,1821

Chase's boat

JUAN FERNANDEZ
ISLANDS

Valparaiso

MÁS AFUERA ISLAND
ESSEX stops for
wood and fish

SANTIAGO

rd boat lost
Jan.28,1921

ST. MARY ISLAND

ESSEX stops for
whaling news
Jan.17,1820

Pollard and
Ramsdell rescued
Feb.23,1821

40°

N

W   E

ATLANTIC OCEAN

S

50°

Dec.18,1819
ESSEX starts passage
around Cape Horn
Heavy gales and seas.

CAPE HORN

100°   90°   80°   70°

The Wreck
of the
Whaleship *Essex*

A Narrative Account by
Owen Chase, First Mate

Edited by Iola Haverstick and Betty Shepard

Introduction by Gary Kinder

A HARVEST BOOK
HARCOURT BRACE & COMPANY
San Diego   New York   London

Library of Congress Catalog Card Number 65-12332

ISBN 0-15-600689-8

Text set in Fairfield Medium
Book designed by Kaelin Chappell
Printed in the United States of America
First Harvest edition 1999

A C E D B

INTRODUCTION

*There is no knowing what a stretch of pain and misery
the human mind is capable of contemplating when
it is wrought upon by the anxieties of preservation,
nor what pangs and weaknesses the body is able
to endure until they are visited upon it.*

OWEN CHASE,
first mate, the whaleship *Essex*

The whale circled away from the *Essex* like an enraged bull, then turned to face it again. Owen Chase could see it thrashing the water into foam, snapping its jaws together "as if distracted with rage and fury." Less than a minute earlier, it had rammed its blunt, massive head into the ship's bow just forward of the chains, and the ship had trembled no less than if it had struck rock. Water was seeping into the hold. Chase had quickly regained his footing but not his senses. Neither he nor anyone else on board could believe that a whale would attack a ship. For over a century the whalemen of Nantucket had passed down the lore of the hunt, and in all of that lore, no whalemen had ever reported being attacked by their prey. The event would have become a part of the lore, perhaps the first of the sea stories recalled whenever whalemen gathered. Chase thought the ramming by the whale could not have been purposeful, but now as he watched, the whale started again toward the ship, pushing a wall of white foam "with tenfold fury and vengeance in his aspect."

Chase and nineteen other men had left Nantucket aboard the *Essex* in August of 1819 for a two-and-a-half-year voyage into the Pacific Ocean in search of whales. For five weeks, heavy gales had slowed their rounding of Cape Horn, and by the time they entered the Pacific and headed up the coast of South America, the New Year had come and gone. For the next eight months they plied the waters off Chile and Peru, harpooning whales. They had taken over twenty-five and filled eight hundred barrels with their prized oil. When the migration slowed, they sailed for the Galápagos, loaded a few hundred turtles for a fresh food supply, then proceeded due west along the equator.

The morning the whale attacked, the crew had set out from the *Essex* in three whaleboats and were pursuing a shoal of whales in the Pacific's equatorial waters. With Chase standing at the bow of his boat, harpoon in hand, four men rowed and another manned the tiller, guiding the boat into the shoal. Chase thrust the harpoon into the first mound of whale flesh to break the surface, but the huge creature twisted toward the boat, driving its tail through the hull near the waterline, then plunged away fast. Chase grabbed the hatchet and cut the line to the harpoon, then stuffed the crew's jackets into the hole, told one man to bail, and ordered the others to row with all haste for the ship. It was the second time in four days that Chase had nearly been killed in a shoal. The first time, one swipe of a fluke had crushed the bottom of his boat and thrown Chase and five others into the air.

"Thus it happens very frequently in the whaling business," Chase wrote later, "that boats are stove, oars, harpoons, and lines broken, ankles and wrists sprained, boats upset, and whole crews left for hours in the water. . . . It is this danger and hardship that makes the sailor; indeed, it is the distinguishing qualification amongst us; and it is a common boast of the whaleman that he has escaped from sudden and apparently inevitable destruction oftener than his fellow."

When they got to the ship, Chase had the damaged boat hoisted from the water. Then he ordered sail raised on the ship's main yard to bring the ship closer to the other two whaleboats, which by now were far to the lee, still in pursuit of the shoal. He had just begun nailing canvas over the hole in his boat, when he saw the big sperm whale surface about a hundred yards from the ship.

The whale swam at the ship for the second time, traveling at about six knots toward the bow, which cut through the water at three knots, and the whale did not alter its course, but rammed its broad head into the bow again with such force that the thick timbers, which for nearly twenty-five years had withstood the fury of the sea around Hope and Horn, cracked and splintered and buckled, and by the time the spray sent skyward descended again, water was gushing into the hold.

As he watched the first attack and now the second, Chase had no idea that the retelling of these moments would later inspire a young writer named Herman Melville to envision a story about a whaling captain and a rogue whale; Chase had other, more immediate, concerns. From the time he first saw the whale, no more than ten minutes had passed before the whale had crashed into the ship twice, he and the crew had launched the spare whaleboat, and the ship had a hole in its bow as big as the captain's quarters. Chase and the five other men were but fifty feet from the *Essex,* when she rolled over on her beam ends and settled in the water.

When the two other boats returned and the crews saw their ship rolled over on its side, the captain at first could not speak. Eventually, he ordered the men back to the ship to save whatever provisions they could. Before the sinking, the steward had gone down to the cabin twice to rescue two compasses, two quadrants, and two practical navigators, so they could navigate celestially. By midafternoon, twenty men hunkered in three lightweight, clinker-built whaleboats, each boat supplied with two hundred pounds of hard bread and sixty-five gallons of drinking water. Their island, their home away from Nantucket, providing dry sleeping quarters and laden with fresh water and fresh turtle and ample provisions, plus the bounty of whale oil from the first year of their voyage, lay overturned on the sea a thousand miles from salvation.

That night, as the whaleboats bobbed in a line fastened to the still-floating ship, Chase reflected on their plight. "How many long and watchful nights, thought I, are to be passed? How many tedious days of partial starvation are to be endured before the least relief or mitigation of our sufferings can be reasonably anticipated?" They had gone from the expectation of adding to the rich haul of oil already in the hold to facing an imminent and violent death or, worse, a slow, painful death. And mixed in with all of their terror and confusion must have been feelings of mortality and thoughts that loved ones would never know what had happened to them. "I have no language to paint the horrors of our situation," wrote Chase. "To shed tears was indeed altogether unavailing and withal unmanly; yet I was not able to deny myself the relief they served to afford me." As he realized their situation, this man, who hours earlier had stood poised at the bow of his boat with a powerful shoulder and forearm raising a harpoon, who could boast that he had escaped from sudden and apparently inevitable destruction oftener than his fellow, dropped his head to his knees and wept.

At noon that first day, the captain took an observation—latitude 0° 40' south, longitude 119° west. He figured their best chance of survival was to rig small sails on each boat and shape their course to the south as far as latitude 25°, the area of the variable winds, then make their way eastward to Chile or Peru. He and Chase calculated that with the trade winds they could make about one degree distance each day, so about twenty-five or twenty-six days down to the variable winds, and no more than thirty days from there to the west coast of South America. Next they calculated how little each man could consume and remain alive, and they predicted that if they rationed carefully, their provisions would last for sixty days. But their calculations proved wrong. And one thing they couldn't know and therefore couldn't ration was the depth of each man's will. How many days could a man absorb the psychological demons that attacked at night when he sat at sea in a tiny boat surrounded by endless stretches of the dark and unknown? For the next three months, they were beset by gales, becalmed in heat, and besieged by the agony that invaded their minds as they floated delicately upon a watery mass that had the power at any moment to rise up and crush the thin shell that separated them from certain death.

Great stories are timeless. They reveal constants of the human condition. The most intriguing and often frightening pull us inside the will to survive, revealing to us things about ourselves that perhaps we would rather not know. The most remarkable aspect of the story of the *Essex* crew was the discipline exhibited by these men in the face of death. Each day each man received a biscuit weighing a little over one pound, and half a pint of fresh water, far below their daily need. This presented a dilemma few of us will ever face, one eloquently described by Chase: "It required a great effort to bring matters to this dreadful alternative: either to feed our bodies—and our hopes—a little longer or, in the agonies of hunger, to seize upon and devour our provisions and then coolly to await the approach of death."

Yet as they grew thinner, they chose not to succumb to their cravings. They hoped that with the smaller rations they might survive a short while longer and that during that tiny window of time rescue would come. As the calculations proved incorrect and time dragged on, they even decided that half of their rations would do, and then decided that half of that was enough, and despite the hunger and the suffering that drove them slowly, inevitably toward death, with only one exception did anyone violate this code of rationing. Chase's hunger reached such an extreme that one night he fell asleep and dreamed of a richly laden banquet table and awakened suddenly so crazed that he seized a patch of cowhide fastened to one of the oars and began to chew it. But each day he would consume no more than his biscuit and his cupful of water.

Ultimately, such discipline saved the lives of five men in the whaleboat. The other twelve lacked either the final stroke of luck or the last drop of fortitude. Those who survived watched the others die. The spirit of one man in Chase's boat departed quietly one afternoon. "For the last three days," wrote Chase, "he had been lying, utterly dispirited and broken down, between the seats in the boat, without being able to do the least duty or hardly to place his hand to his head. This morning he had made up his mind to die rather than to endure further misery. He refused his allowance of bread, said he was sensible of his approaching end and was perfectly ready to die. In a few minutes he became speechless. The breath appeared to be leaving his body without producing the least pain. At four o'clock he was gone. . . . The next morning we committed him to the sea."

The next one did not go so peacefully. "He lay in the greatest pain and apparent misery," recalled Chase, "groaning piteously until four o'clock in the afternoon, when he died in the most horrid and frightful convulsions I ever witnessed. We kept his corpse all night. In the morning my two companions began, as a matter of course, to make preparations to dispose of it in the sea when, having reflected on the subject all night, I addressed them on [a] painful subject. . . . Our provisions could not possibly last us beyond three days."

What you are about to read is at once the most fundamental and the most horrifying experience you can imagine. Yet, had you been there, reduced to the level these men were, is there any doubt that you, too, would have become so desperate as to drink your own urine? Is there any doubt that you would have cut open the chest of a dead shipmate and eaten his heart and reflected only later on the horrific experience that had driven you to that precise point where the opportunity to sustain yourself a few days longer prevailed over the repulsion of eating the flesh of a comrade whose constitution had fallen just short of yours?

Light a fire, pour yourself a glass of port, settle back into that overstuffed leather chair, and let the most amazing story in the annals of the sea transport you to a different time, a different breed, an experience few could believe, let alone imagine. As you sit in your chair, the subliminal thought recurs: My god, this really happened.

GARY KINDER
June 1999

The Wreck
of the
Whaleship *Essex*

*"We made the longitude of the Cape
about the 18th of December."*

The town of Nantucket, in the State of Massachusetts, contains about eight thousand inhabitants. Nearly a third part of the population are Quakers, and they are, taken together, a very industrious and enterprising people.

On this island are owned about one hundred vessels, of all descriptions, engaged in the whale trade, giving constant employment and support to upwards of sixteen hundred hardy seamen, a class of people proverbial for their intrepidity. This fishery is not carried on to any extent from any other part of the United States, except from the town of New Bedford, directly opposite to Nantucket on the mainland, where are owned probably twenty sail.

A voyage generally lasts about two years and a half with an entire uncertainty of success. Sometimes the whalemen are repaid with speedy voyages and profitable cargoes, but at others they drag out a listless and disheartening cruise, scarcely making the expenses of an outfit. The business is considered a very hazardous one, arising from unavoidable accidents in carrying on an exterminating warfare against those great leviathans of the deep. Indeed, a Nantucket man is on all occasions fully sensible of the honour and merit of his profession—no doubt because he knows that his laurels, like the soldier's, are plucked from the brink of danger.

Numerous anecdotes are related of the whalemen of Nantucket. Stories of hairbreadth escapes and sudden and wonderful preservation are handed down amongst them with the fidelity—and no doubt with the characteristic fictions—of the ancient legendary tales. A spirit of adventure amongst the sons and other relatives of those immediately concerned in the fishery takes possession of their minds at a very early age. Captivated with the tough stories of the elder seamen and seduced by the natural desire of seeing foreign countries, as well as by the hopes of gain, they launch forth six or eight thousand miles from home into an almost untraversed ocean, where they spend from two to three years of their lives in scenes of constant peril, labour, and watchfulness.

The profession is one of great ambition and is full of honourable excitement. A tame man is never known amongst them, and the coward is marked with that peculiar aversion that distinguishes our public naval service. There are perhaps no people of superior corporeal powers, but it has been truly said that they possess a natural aptitude, which seems rather the lineal spirit of their fathers than the effects of any experience.

The town itself, during the War of 1812, was (naturally to have been expected) on the decline. But with the return of peace, it took a fresh start, and a spirit for carrying on the fishery received a renewed and very considerable excitement. Large amounts of capital are now invested, and some of the finest ships that our country can boast of are employed in it. The increased demand, within a few years past, from the spermaceti candle manufactories has induced companies and individuals in different parts of the Union to become engaged in the business. If the future consumption of the manufactured article should bear any proportion to that of the few past years, this species of commerce will bid fair to become the most profitable and extensive that our country possesses. From the accounts of those who were concerned with the early stages of the fishery, it would appear that the whales have been driven, like the beasts of the forest before the march of civilization, into remote and more unfrequented seas until now they are followed by the enterprise and perseverance of our seamen even to the distant coasts of Japan.

The ship *Essex*, commanded by Captain George Pollard, Junior, was fitted out at Nantucket. She sailed on the 12th day of August, 1819, for the Pacific Ocean on a whaling voyage. Of this ship I was first mate. She had lately undergone a thorough repair in her upper works and was at that time, in all respects, a sound, substantial vessel. She had a crew of twenty men and was victualled and provided for two years and a half.

We left the coast of America with a fine breeze and steered for the Western Islands. On the second day out, while sailing moderately on our course in the Gulf Stream, a sudden squall of wind struck the ship from the southwest and knocked her completely on her beam-ends, stove one of our boats, entirely destroyed two others, and threw down the cambouse.

We distinctly saw the approach of this gust but miscalculated altogether as to the strength and violence of it. It struck the ship about three points off the weather quarter, at the moment that the man at the helm was in the act of putting her away to run before it. In an instant she was knocked down with her yards in the water; however, before hardly a moment of time was allowed for reflection, she gradually came to the wind and righted. The squall was accompanied with vivid flashes of lightning and heavy and repeated claps of thunder. The whole ship's crew were, for a short time, thrown into the utmost consternation and confusion, but fortunately the violence of the squall was all contained in the first gust of the wind. It soon gradually abated and became fine weather again. We repaired our damage with little difficulty and continued on our course with the loss of the two boats.

On the 30th of August we made the island of Flores, one of the Western group called the Azores. We lay off and on the island for two days, during which time our boats landed and obtained a supply of vegetables and a few hogs. From this place we took the northeast trade wind and, in sixteen days, made the isle of May, one of the Cape Verde group. As we were sailing along the shore of this island, we discovered a ship stranded on the beach and, from her appearance, took her to be a whaler. Having lost two of our boats and presuming that this vessel had probably some belonging to her that might have been saved, we determined to ascertain the name of the ship and to endeavour to supply if possible the loss of our boats from her. We accordingly stood in towards the port or landing place. After a short time three men were discovered coming out to us in a whaleboat. In a few moments they were alongside. They informed us that the wreck was the *Archimedes* of New York, Captain George B. Coffin. This vessel had struck on a rock near the island about a fortnight previously. All hands were saved by running the ship on shore, and the captain and crew had since gone home. We purchased the whaleboat of these people, obtained some few more pigs, and again set sail.

Our passage thence to Cape Horn was not distinguished for any incident worthy of note. We made the longitude of the Cape about the 18th of December, having experienced head winds for nearly the whole distance. We anticipated a moderate time in passing this noted land, as the season of the year at which we were there was considered the most favourable. But instead of this, we experienced heavy westerly gales and a most tremendous sea that detained us off the Cape five weeks before we had got sufficiently to the westward to enable us to put away.

Of the passage of this famous cape, it may be observed that strong westerly gales and a heavy sea are its almost universal attendants. The prevalence and constancy of this wind and sea necessarily produce a rapid current, by which vessels are set to leeward; and it is not without some favourable slant of wind that they can, in many cases, get round at all. The difficulties and dangers of the passage are proverbial; but as far as my own observation extends—and which the numerous reports of the whalemen corroborate—you can always rely upon a long and regular sea. Although the gales may be very strong and stubborn, as they undoubtedly are, they are not known to blow with the destructive violence that characterizes some of the tornadoes of the western Atlantic Ocean.

On the 17th of January, 1820, we arrived at the island of St. Mary, which lies off the coast of Chili in latitude 36° 59′

south, longitude 73° 41′ west. This island is a sort of rendezvous for whalers; from it they obtain their food and water, and between it and the mainland—a distance of about ten miles—they frequently cruise for a species of whale called the right whale. Our object in going in there was merely to get the news.

We sailed thence to the island of Más Afuera, where we got some wood and fish, and thence for the cruising ground along the coast of Chili in search of the spermaceti whale. We took eight, which yielded us two hundred and fifty barrels of oil. The season there having by this time expired, we changed our cruising ground to the coast of Peru, where we obtained five hundred and fifty barrels.

After going into a small port and replenishing our wood and water, we set sail on the 2nd of October for the Galápagos Islands. We came to anchor and laid seven days off Hood Island, one of the group. During this time we stopped a leak which we had discovered and obtained three hundred turtle. We then visited Charles Island, where we procured sixty more.

These turtle are a most delicious food. They average in weight generally about one hundred pounds, but many of them weigh upwards of eight hundred. With these, ships usually supply themselves for a great length of time and make a great saving of other provisions. They neither eat nor drink, nor is the least pains taken with them. They are strewed over the deck, thrown under foot, or packed away in the hold, as it suits convenience. They will live upwards of a year without food or water, but soon die in a cold climate.

We left Charles Island on the 23rd of October and steered off to the westward in search of whales. In latitude 1° 0′ south, longitude 180° west, on the 16th of November, in the afternoon, we lost a boat during our work in a shoal of whales. I was in the boat myself, with five others, and was standing in the fore part with the harpoon in my hand, well braced, expecting every instant to catch sight of one of the shoal which we were in so that I might strike. But judge of my astonishment and dismay at finding myself suddenly thrown up in the air, my companions scattered about me, and the boat fast filling with water. A whale had come up directly under her and, with one dash of his tail, had stove her bottom in and strewed us in every direction around her. We, however, with little difficulty, got safely on the wreck and clung there until one of the other boats which had been engaged in the shoal came to our assistance and took us off.

Strange to tell, not a man was injured by this accident. Thus it happens very frequently in the whaling business that boats are stove, oars, harpoons, and lines broken, ankles and wrists sprained, boats upset, and whole crews left for hours in the water without any of these accidents extending to the loss of life. We are so much accustomed to the continual recurrence of such scenes as these that we become familiarized to them. Consequently, we always feel that confidence and self-possession, which teaches us every expedient in danger, and which inures the body, as well as the mind, to fatigue, privation, and peril, in frequent cases exceeding belief.

It is this danger and hardship that makes the sailor; indeed, it is the distinguishing qualification amongst us; and it is a common boast of the whaleman that he has escaped from sudden and apparently inevitable destruction oftener than his fellow. He is accordingly valued on this account without much reference to other qualities.

"My God, Mr. Chase,
what is the matter?"

I have not been able to recur to the scenes which are now to become the subject of description, although a considerable time has elapsed, without feeling a mingled emotion of horror and astonishment at the almost incredible destiny that has preserved me and my surviving companions from a terrible death.

Frequently, in my reflections on the subject, even after this lapse of time, I find myself shedding tears of gratitude for our deliverance and blessing God, by whose divine aid and protection we were conducted through a series of unparalleled suffering and distress and restored to the bosoms of our families and friends.

There is no knowing what a stretch of pain and misery the human mind is capable of contemplating when it is wrought upon by the anxieties of preservation, nor what pangs and weaknesses the body is able to endure until they are visited upon it. And when at last deliverance comes, when the dream of hope is realized, unspeakable gratitude takes possession of the soul, and tears of joy choke the utterance. We require to be taught in the school of some signal suffering, privation, and despair the great lessons of constant dependence upon an Almighty forbearance and mercy. In the midst of the wide ocean at night, when the sight of the heavens was shut out and the dark tempest came upon us, then it was that we felt ourselves ready to exclaim: "Heaven have mercy upon us, for nought but that can save us now."

But I proceed to the recital. On the 20th of November (cruising in latitude 0° 40′ south, longitude 119° 0′ west), a shoal of whales was discovered off the lee bow. The weather at this time was extremely fine and clear; it was about eight o'clock in the morning that the man at the masthead gave the usual cry of "There she blows." The ship was immediately put away, and we ran down in the direction for them. When we had got within half a mile of the place where they were observed, all our boats were lowered down, manned, and we started in pursuit of the shoal. The ship, in the meantime, was brought to the wind and the main topsail hove aback to wait for us. I had the harpoon in the second boat; the captain preceded me in the first.

When I arrived at the spot where we calculated they were, nothing was at first to be seen. We lay on our oars in anxious expectation of discovering them come up somewhere near us. Presently one rose and spouted a short distance ahead of my boat. I made all speed towards him, came up with him, and struck him. Feeling the harpoon, he threw himself in an agony over towards the boat (which at that time was up alongside of him), and giving a severe blow with his tail, struck the boat near the edge of the water, amidships, and stove a hole in her. I immediately took up the boat hatchet and cut the line from the harpoon to disengage the boat from the whale, which by this time was running off with great velocity. I succeeded in getting clear of him, with the loss of the harpoon and line, and finding the water to pour fast in the boat, I hastily stuffed three or four of our jackets in the hole, ordered one man to keep constantly bailing and the rest to pull immediately for the ship. We succeeded in keeping the boat free and shortly gained the ship. The captain and the second mate, in the other two boats, kept up the pursuit and soon struck another whale. They being at this time a considerable distance to leeward, I went forward, braced around the main yard, and put the ship off in a direction for them.

The boat which had been stove was immediately hoisted in, and after examining the hole, I found that I could, by nailing a piece of canvas over it, get her ready to join in a fresh pursuit sooner than by lowering down the other remaining boat which belonged to the ship. I accordingly turned her over upon the quarter and was in the act of nailing on the canvas when I observed a very large spermaceti whale, as well as I could judge about eighty-five feet in length. He broke water about twenty rods off our weather bow and was lying quietly, with his head in a direction for the ship. He spouted two or three times and then disappeared. In less than two or three seconds, he came up again, about the length of the ship off, and made directly for us at the rate of about three knots. The ship was then going with about the same velocity. His appearance and attitude gave us at first no alarm, but while I stood watching his movements and observing him, but a ship's length off, coming down for us with great celerity, I involuntarily ordered the boy at the helm to put it hard up, intending to sheer off and avoid him.

The words were scarcely out of my mouth before he came down upon us with full speed and struck the ship with his head, just forward of the fore-chains. He gave us such an appalling and tremendous jar as nearly threw us all on our faces. The ship brought up as suddenly and violently as if she had struck a rock and trembled for a few seconds like a leaf.

We looked at each other with perfect amazement, deprived almost of the power of speech. Many minutes elapsed before we were able to realize the dreadful accident. During this time the whale passed under the ship, grazing her keel as he went along. He came up alongside of her to leeward and lay on the top of the water, apparently stunned with the violence of the blow, for the space of a minute. He then suddenly started off in a direction to leeward.

After a few moments' reflection and recovering, in some measure, from the sudden consternation that had seized us, I of course concluded that he had stove a hole in the ship and that it would be necessary to set the pumps going. Accordingly, they were rigged but had not been in operation more than one minute before I perceived the head of the ship to be gradually settling down in the water. I then ordered the signal to be set for the other boats, which scarcely had I dispatched before I again discovered the whale, apparently in convulsions, on the top of the water about one hundred rods to leeward. He was enveloped in the foam of the sea that his continual and violent thrashing about in the water had created around him, and I could distinctly see him smite his jaws together, as if distracted with rage and fury. He remained a short time in this situation and then started off with great velocity across the bow of the ship to windward.

By this time the ship had settled down a considerable distance in the water, and I gave her up as lost. I, however, ordered the pumps to be kept constantly going and endeavoured to collect my thoughts for the occasion. I turned to the boats, two of which we then had with the ship, with an intention of clearing them away and getting all things ready to embark in them if there should be no other resource left. While my attention was thus engaged for a moment, I was aroused with the cry of a man at the hatchway: "Here he is— he is making for us again."

I turned around and saw him, about one hundred rods directly ahead of us, coming down apparently with twice his ordinary speed and, it appeared to me at that moment, with tenfold fury and vengeance in his aspect. The surf flew in all directions about him, and his course towards us was marked by white foam a rod in width, which he made with the continual violent thrashing of his tail. His head was about half out of water, and in that way he came upon and again struck the ship.

I was in hopes, when I descried him making for us, that, by a dexterous movement of putting the ship away immediately, I should be able to cross the line of his approach before he could get up to us and thus avoid what I knew, if he should strike us again, would prove our inevitable destruction. I bawled out to the helmsman, "Hard up!" But she had not fallen off more than a point before we took the second shock. I should judge the speed of the ship to have been at this time about three knots and that of the whale about six. He struck her to windward, directly under the cathead, and completely stove in her bow. He passed under the ship again, went off to leeward, and we saw no more of him.

Our situation at this juncture can be more readily imagined than described. The shock to our feelings was such as I am sure none can have an adequate conception of that were not there. The misfortune befell us at a moment when we least dreamt of any accident. From the pleasing anticipations we had formed of realizing the certain profits of our labour, we were dejected by a sudden, most mysterious, and overwhelming calamity.

Not a moment, however, was to be lost in endeavouring to provide for the extremity to which it was now certain we were reduced. We were more than a thousand miles from the nearest land with nothing but a light open boat as the resource of safety for myself and companions. I ordered the men to cease pumping and everyone to provide for himself. Seizing a hatchet at the same time, I cut away the lashings of the spare boat, which lay, bottom up, across two spars directly over the quarterdeck, and cried out to those near me to take her as she came down. They did so, accordingly, and bore her on their shoulders as far as the waist of the ship.

The steward had in the meantime gone down into the cabin twice and saved two quadrants, two practical navigators, and the captain's trunk and mine. All of these were hastily thrown into the boat as she lay on the deck, along with the two compasses which I snatched from the binnacle. The steward attempted to descend again, but the water by this time had rushed in, and he returned without being able to effect his purpose. By the time we had got the boat to the waist, the ship had filled with water and was going down on her beam-ends. We shoved our boat as quickly as possible from the plank-sheer into the water, all hands jumping in her at the same time, and we launched off clear of the ship. We were scarcely two boat lengths distant from her when she fell over to windward and settled down in the water.

Amazement and despair now wholly took possession of us. We contemplated the frightful situation the ship lay in and thought with horror upon the sudden and dreadful calamity that had overtaken us. We looked upon each other, as if to gather some consolatory sensation from an interchange of sentiments, but every countenance was marked with the paleness of despair. Not a word was spoken for several minutes by any of us; all appeared to be bound in a spell of stupid consternation.

From the time we were first attacked by the whale to the period of the fall of the ship and of our leaving her in the boat, more than ten minutes could not certainly have elapsed! God only knows in what way or by what means we were enabled to accomplish in that short time what we did. The cutting away and transporting of the boat from where she was deposited would of itself, in ordinary circumstances, have consumed as much time as that if the whole ship's crew had been employed in it. My companions had not saved a single article but what they had on their backs. But to me it was a source of infinite satisfaction, if any such could be gathered from the horrors of our gloomy situation, that we had been fortunate enough to have preserved our compasses, navigators, and quadrants. After the first shock of my feelings was over, I enthusiastically contemplated them as the probable instruments of our salvation; without them all would have been dark and hopeless.

Gracious God, what a picture of distress and suffering

now presented itself to my imagination! The crew of the ship—consisting of twenty human souls—were saved. All that remained to conduct these twenty beings through the stormy terrors of the ocean, perhaps many thousand miles, were three open light boats. The prospect of obtaining any provisions or water from the ship to subsist upon during the time was at least now doubtful.

How many long and watchful nights, thought I, are to be passed? How many tedious days of partial starvation are to be endured before the least relief or mitigation of our sufferings can be reasonably anticipated?

We lay at this time in our boat—about two ship lengths off from the wreck—in perfect silence, calmly contemplating her situation and absorbed in our own melancholy reflections, when the other boats were discovered rowing up to us. They had but shortly before discovered that some accident had befallen us, but of the nature of it they were entirely ignorant. The sudden and mysterious disappearance of the ship was first discovered by the boat-steerer in the captain's boat. With a horror-struck countenance and voice, he suddenly exclaimed: "Oh, my God! Where is the ship?"

Upon this, their operations were instantly suspended, and a general cry of horror and despair burst from the lips of every man, as their looks were directed for the ship, in vain, over every part of the ocean.

They immediately made all haste towards us. The captain's boat was the first that reached us. He stopped about a boat's length off but had no power to utter a single syllable. He was so completely overpowered with the spectacle before him that he sat down in his boat, pale and speechless. He appeared to be so much altered, awed, and overcome with the oppression of his feelings and the dreadful reality that lay before him that I could scarcely recognize his countenance. He was in a short time, however, enabled to address an inquiry to me. "My God, Mr. Chase, what is the matter?"

I answered: "We have been stove by a whale." I then briefly told him the story. After a few moments' reflection, he observed that we must cut away her masts and endeavour to get something out of her to eat.

Our thoughts were now all accordingly bent on endeavours to save from the wreck whatever we might possibly want, and for this purpose we rowed up and got onto her. Search was made for every means of gaining access to her hold. For this purpose the lanyards were cut loose, and with our hatchets we commenced to cut away the masts so that she might right up again and enable us to scuttle her decks. In doing this, we were occupied about three quarters of an hour, owing to our having no axes nor indeed any other instruments but the small hatchets belonging to the boats. After her masts were gone, she came up about two-thirds of the way upon an even keel.

While we were employed about the masts, the captain took his quadrant, shoved off from the ship, and got an observation. We found ourselves in latitude 0° 40′ south, longitude 119° west.

We now commenced to cut a hole through the planks directly above two large casks of bread, which most fortunately were between decks in the waist of the ship. As these were on the upper side when the ship upset, we had strong hopes they were not wet. It turned out according to our wishes, and from these casks we obtained six hundred pounds of hard bread. Other parts of the deck were then scuttled, and we got without difficulty as much fresh water as we dared to take in the boats, so that each was supplied with about sixty-five gallons. We got also from one of the lockers a musket, a small canister of powder, a couple of files, two rasps, about two pounds of boat nails, and a few turtle.

In the afternoon the wind came on to blow a strong breeze. Having obtained everything that occurred to us that could then be got out, we began to make arrangements for our safety during the night. A boat's line was made fast to the ship, and one of the boats was moored to the other end of it at about fifty fathoms to leeward. Another boat was then attached to the first one about eight fathoms astern, and the third boat was tied the like distance astern of her.

Night came on just as we had finished our operations, and such a night as it was to us—so full of feverish and distracting inquietude that we were deprived entirely of rest! The wreck was constantly before my eyes. I could not, by any effort, chase away the horrors of the preceding day from my mind. They haunted me the livelong night. My companions—some of them were like sick women—had no idea of the extent of their deplorable situation. One or two slept unconcernedly, while others wasted the night in unavailing murmurs.

I now had full leisure to examine with some degree of coolness the dreadful circumstances of our disaster. The scenes of yesterday passed in such quick succession in my mind that it was not until after many hours of severe reflection that I was able to discard the idea of the catastrophe as a dream. Alas, it was one from which there was no awaking! It was too certainly true that but yesterday we had existed, as it were, and in one short moment had been cut off from all the hopes and prospects of the living! I have no language to paint the horrors of our situation. To shed tears was indeed altogether unavailing and withal unmanly; yet I was not able to deny myself the relief they served to afford me.

After several hours of idle sorrow and repining, I began to reflect upon the accident. I endeavoured to realize by what unaccountable destiny or design (which it was I could not at first determine) this sudden and most deadly attack had been made upon us by an animal never before suspected of premeditated violence and proverbial for its insensibility and inoffensiveness. Every fact seemed to warrant me in concluding that it was anything but chance which directed his operations. He made two separate attacks upon the ship within a short interval, both of which, according to their direction, were calculated to do us the most injury. By being made ahead, they thereby combined the speed of the two objects for the shock. To effect this impact, the exact maneuvers which he made were necessary.

His aspect was most horrible and such as indicated resentment and fury. He came directly from the shoal which we had just before entered—and in which we had struck three of his companions—as if he were fired with revenge for their sufferings. But to this it may be observed that the mode of fighting which these whales always adopt is either with repeated strokes of their tails or by snapping of their jaws together, and that a case precisely similar to this one has never been heard of amongst the oldest and most experienced whalers.

To this I would answer that the structure and strength of the whale's head is admirably designed for this mode of attack. The most prominent part of it is almost as hard and as tough as iron; indeed, I can compare it to nothing else but the inside of a horse's hoof, upon which a lance or harpoon would not make the slightest impression. The eyes and ears of the whale are removed nearly one-third the length of the whole fish from the front part of the head and are not in the least degree endangered in this mode of attack. At all events, the whole circumstances taken together, and all happening before my own eyes, produced, at the time impressions in my mind of decided, calculating mischief on the part of the whale and induce me to be satisfied that I am correct in my opinion.

It is certainly, in all its bearings, a hitherto unheard of circumstance and constitutes, perhaps, the most extraordinary one in the annals of the fishery.

"At half past twelve we left the wreck."

NOVEMBER 21ST. The morning dawned upon our wretched company. The weather was fine, but the wind blew a strong breeze from the southeast, and the sea was very rugged. Watches had been kept up during the night, in our respective boats, to see that none of the spars or other articles which continued to float out of the wreck should be thrown by the surf against the boats and injure them.

At sunrise, we began to think of doing something; what, we did not know. We cast loose our boats and visited the wreck to see if anything more of consequence could be preserved, but everything looked cheerless and desolate. We made a long and vain search for any useful article; nothing could be found but a few turtles. Of these we had enough already—or at least as many as could be safely stowed in the boats—and we wandered around in every part of the ship in a sort of vacant idleness for the greater part of the morning.

Presently we were aroused to a perfect sense of our destitute and forlorn condition by thoughts of the means which we had for our subsistence, the necessity of not wasting our time and of endeavouring to seek some relief wherever God might direct us. Our thoughts, indeed, hung about the ship, wrecked and sunken as she was, and we could scarcely discard from our minds the idea of her continuing protection. Some great efforts in our situation were necessary, and a great deal of calculation was important as it concerned the means by which our existence was to be supported during, perhaps, a very long period, as well as a provision for our eventual deliverance. Accordingly, by agreement, all set to work in stripping off the light sails of the ship for sails for our boats. The day was consumed in making them up and fitting them.

We furnished ourselves with masts and other light spars that were necessary from the wreck. Each boat was rigged with two masts—to carry a flying jib and two spritsails. The spritsails were made so that two reefs could be taken in them in case of heavy blows. We continued to watch the wreck for any serviceable articles that might float from her and kept one man during the day on the stump of her foremast, on the lookout for vessels.

Our work was very much impeded by the increase of the wind and sea, and the surf, breaking almost continually into the boats, gave us many fears that we should not be able to prevent our provisions from getting wet. Above all, it served to increase the constant apprehensions that we had of the insufficiency of the boats themselves during the rough weather that we should necessarily experience. In order to provide as much as possible against this—and withal to strengthen the slight materials of which the boats were constructed—we procured from the wreck some light cedar boards, intended to repair boats in cases of accidents, with which we built up additional sides about six inches above the gunwale. These, we afterwards found, were of infinite service for the purpose for which they were intended; in truth, I am satisfied we could never have been preserved without them. The boats must otherwise have taken in so much water that all the efforts of twenty such weak, starving men, as we afterwards came to be, would not have sufficed to keep them free.

But what appeared most immediately to concern us and to command all our anxieties was the security of our provisions from the salt water. We disposed of them under a covering of wood that whaleboats have at either end of them, after wrapping them up in several thicknesses of canvas.

I got an observation today, by which I found we were in latitude 0° 6′ south, longitude 119° 30′ west, having been driven by the winds a distance of forty-nine miles the last twenty-four hours. By this it would appear that there must have been a strong current, setting us to the northwest during the whole time.

We were not able to finish our sails in one day. Many little things preparatory to taking a final leave of the ship were necessary to be attended to, but evening came and put an end to our labours. We made the same arrangements for mooring the boats in safety and consigned ourselves to the horrors of another tempestuous night. The wind continued to blow hard, keeping up a heavy sea and veering around from southeast to east and east-southeast. As the gloom of night approached and obliged us to desist from that employment, which, by occupying us, cheated us out of some of the realities of our situation, we all of us again became mute and desponding. The preceding day a considerable degree of alacrity had been manifested by many as their attention had been wholly engaged in scrutinizing the wreck and in constructing the sails and spars for the boats. But when they ceased to be occupied, they passed to a sudden fit of melancholy, and the miseries of their situation came upon them with such force as to produce spells of extreme debility, approaching almost to fainting.

Our provisions were scarcely touched—appetite was entirely gone. But as we had a great abundance of water, we indulged in frequent and copious draughts, which our parched mouths seemed continually to need. No one asked for bread. Our continued state of anxiety during the night excluded all hopes of sleep. Although the solemn fact had been before me for nearly two days, my mind still manifested the utmost repugnance to be reconciled to it.

I lay down in the bottom of the boat and resigned myself to reflection. My silent prayers were offered up to the God of mercy for that protection which we stood so much in need of. Sometimes, indeed, a light hope would dawn. But then, to feel such an utter dependence on and consignment to chance alone for aid and rescue would chase it again from my mind. The wreck—the mysterious and mortal attack of the animal—the sudden prostration and sinking of the vessel—our escape from her—and our then forlorn and almost hapless destiny—all passed in quick and perplexing review in my imagination.

Wearied with the exertion of body and mind, I caught, near morning, an hour's respite from my troubles in sleep.

NOVEMBER 22ND. The wind remained the same, and the weather continued remarkably fine. At sunrise, we again hauled our boats up to the wreck and continued our search for articles that might float out. About seven o'clock, the deck of the wreck began to give way, and every appearance indicated her speedy dissolution. The oil had bilged in the hold and kept the surface of the sea all around us completely covered with it. The bulkheads were all washed down, and she worked in every part of her joints and seams with the violent and continual breaking of the surf over her.

Seeing, at last, that little or nothing further could be done by remaining with the wreck, and as it was all important that while our provisions lasted we should make the best possible use of time, I rowed up to the captain's boat and asked him what he intended to do. I informed him that the ship's decks had bursted up and that, in all probability, she would soon go to pieces, that no further purpose could be answered by remaining longer with her, since nothing more could be obtained from her, and that it was my opinion no time should be lost in making the best of our way towards the nearest land.

The captain replied that he would go once more to the wreck and survey her and, after waiting until twelve o'clock for the purpose of getting an observation, would immediately thereafter make a decision. In the meantime, before noon, all our sails were completed and the boats otherwise got in readiness for our departure. As near as we could determine it, our observation now proved us to be in latitude 0° 13′ north, longitude 120° 00′ west. We had crossed the equator during the night and drifted nineteen miles. The wind had veered considerably to the eastward during the last twenty-four hours.

Our nautical calculations having been completed, the captain, after visiting the wreck, called a council, consisting of himself and the first and second mates, who all repaired to his boat to interchange opinions and to devise the best means for our security and preservation. There were, in all of us, twenty men, six of whom were blacks, and we had three boats. We examined our navigators to ascertain the nearest land and found it was the Marquesas Islands. The Society Islands were next, but we were entirely ignorant of these islands. If inhabited, we presumed it was by savages— from whom we had as much to fear as from the elements, or even death itself.

We had no charts from which our calculations might be aided and were, consequently, obliged to govern ourselves by the navigators alone. It was also the captain's opinion that this was the season of the hurricanes which prevail in the vicinity of the Sandwich Islands and that, consequently, it would be unsafe to steer for them. The issue of our deliberations was that, taking all things into consideration, it would be most advisable to shape our course by the wind to the southward as far as the latitude of 25° or 26°, to fall in there with the variable winds, and then to endeavour to get eastward to the coast of Chili or Peru. Accordingly, preparations were made for our immediate departure.

The boat which it was my fortune, or rather misfortune, to have was the worst of the three. She was old and patched up, having been stove a number of times during the cruise. At best, a whaleboat is an extremely frail thing—the most so of any other kind of boat. They are what is called clinker built and are constructed of the lightest materials for the purpose of being rowed with the greatest possible celerity, which is according to the necessities of the business for which they are intended. Of all species of vessels, they are the weakest and most fragile and possess but one advantage over any other—that of lightness and buoyancy, which enables them to keep above the dash of the sea with more facility than heavier vessels. This qualification is, however, preferable to that of any other, and situated as we then were, I would not have exchanged her, old and crazy as she was, for even a ship's launch. I am quite confident that to this quality of our boats we most especially owed our preservation through the many days and nights of heavy weather that we afterwards encountered.

In consideration of my having the weakest boat, six men were allotted to it, while those of the captain and second mate took seven each. At half past twelve we left the wreck, steering our course, with nearly all sail set, south-southeast.

At four o'clock in the afternoon we lost sight of her entirely. Many were the lingering and sorrowful looks we cast behind us.

"The water flew all over us."

It has appeared to me often since to have been, in the abstract, an extreme weakness and folly on our parts to have looked upon our shattered and sunken vessel with such an excessive fondness and regret. But it seemed as if in abandoning her, we had parted with all hope and were bending our course away from her by some dictate of despair.

We agreed to keep together in our boats, as nearly as possible, to afford assistance in cases of accident and to render our reflections less melancholy by each other's presence. I found it on this occasion true that misery does indeed love company. Unaided and unencouraged by each other, there were with us many whose weak minds, I am confident, would have sunk under the dismal retrospections of the past catastrophe and who did not possess either sense or firmness enough to contemplate our approaching destiny without the cheering of some more determined countenance than their own.

The wind was strong all day, and the sea ran very high. Our boat took in water from her leaks continually, so that we were obliged to keep one man constantly bailing. During the night the weather became extremely rugged, and the sea every now and then broke over us. By agreement, we were divided into two watches, one of which was to be constantly awake, doing the labours of the boat, such as bailing, setting, taking in, and trimming the sails.

We kept our course very well together during this night and had many opportunities of conversation with the men in the other boats, wherein the means and prospects of our deliverance were variously considered. It appeared from the opinions of all that we had most to hope for in the meeting with some vessel—most probably some whaleship. The great majority of those vessels in these seas were, we imagined, cruising about the latitude we were then steering for. But this was only a hope, the realization of which did not in any degree depend on our own exertions but on chance alone. It was not, therefore, considered prudent to go out of our course with the prospect of meeting them or to lose sight for one moment of the strong probabilities which, under Divine Providence, there were of our reaching land by the route we had prescribed for ourselves and that depended most especially on a reasonable calculation and on our own labours.

We conceived that our provisions and water, on a small allowance, would last us sixty days and that, with the trade wind on the course we were then lying, we should be able to average the distance of a degree a day. In twenty-six days, this would enable us to attain the region of the variable winds, and then, in thirty more days, at the very utmost—should there be any favour in the elements—we might reach the coast. With these considerations we commenced our voyage, the total failure of which, and the subsequent dismal distress and suffering by which we were overtaken, will be shown in the sequel.

Our allowance of provisions at first consisted of bread, one biscuit weighing about one pound three ounces, and half a pint of water a day for each man. This small quantity was less than one-third of that which is required by an ordinary person. Small as it was, however, we took it without murmuring and on many an occasion afterwards blest God that even this pittance was allowed to us in our misery.

The darkness of another night overtook us, and after having for the first time partook of our allowance of bread and water, we laid our weary bodies down in the boat and endeavoured to get some repose. Nature became at last worn out with the watchings and anxieties of the two preceding nights, and sleep came insensibly upon us. No dreams could break the strong fastenings of forgetfulness in which the mind was then locked up.

But for my own part, my thoughts so haunted me that this luxury was yet a stranger to my eyes. Every recollection was still fresh before me, and I enjoyed but a few short and unsatisfactory slumbers, caught in the intervals between my hopes and my fears. The dark ocean and swelling waters were nothing. The fears of being swallowed up by some dreadful tempest or dashed upon hidden rocks, together with all the other ordinary subjects of fearful contemplation, seemed scarcely entitled to a moment's thought. Instead, the dismal-looking wreck and the horrid aspect and revenge of the whale wholly engrossed my reflections until day again made its appearance.

NOVEMBER 23RD. In my sea chest, which I was fortunate enough to preserve, I had several small articles which we found of great service to us; among them were some eight or ten sheets of writing paper, a lead pencil, a suit of clothes, three small fishhooks, a jackknife, a whetstone, and a cake of soap.

I commenced to keep a sort of journal with the little paper and pencil which I had, and the knife, besides other useful purposes, served us as a razor. It was with much difficulty, however, that I could keep any sort of record, owing to the incessant rocking and unsteadiness of the boat and the continual dashing of the spray of the sea over us. In addition to the articles enumerated, the boat contained a lantern, a tinderbox, and two or three candles, which belonged to her and with which whaleboats are kept always supplied while engaged in taking whale. In addition to all of this, the captain had saved a musket, two pistols, and a canister containing about two pounds of gunpowder. The latter he distributed equal proportions between the three boats and gave the second mate and myself each a pistol.

When morning came, we found ourselves quite near together. The wind had considerably increased since the day before. We were consequently obliged to reef our sails, and although we did not apprehend any very great danger from the then violence of the wind, it grew to be very uncomfortable in the boats from the repeated dashing of the waves, which kept our bodies constantly wet with the salt spray. We, however, stood along our course until twelve o'clock, when we got an observation—as well as we were able to obtain one while the water flew all over us and the sea kept the boat extremely unsteady. We found ourselves this day in latitude 0° 58′ south, having repassed the equator. We abandoned the idea altogether of keeping any correct longitudinal reckoning, having no glass nor logline.

The wind moderated in the course of the afternoon a little but at night came on to blow again almost a gale. We began now to tremble for our little barque; she was so ill calculated to withstand the racking of the sea, and it required the constant labours of one man to keep her free of water. We were surrounded in the afternoon with porpoises that kept playing about us in great numbers and continued to follow us during the night.

NOVEMBER 24TH. The wind had not abated any since the preceding day, and the sea had risen to be very large and increased, if possible, the extreme uncomfortableness of our situation. What added more than anything else to our misfortunes was that all our efforts for the preservation of our provisions proved, in a great measure, ineffectual. A heavy sea broke suddenly into the boat and, before we could snatch our provisions up, damaged some part of them. By timely attention, however, and great caution, we managed to make them eatable and to preserve the rest from a similar casualty.

This was a subject of extreme anxiety to us. Deprived of our provisions, the expectation upon which our final rescue was founded must change at once to utter hopelessness. Our provisions were the only means of continuing us in the exercise, not only of our manual powers, but also in those of reason itself. Hence, above all other things, this was the object of our utmost solicitude and pains.

We ascertained, the next day, that some of the provisions in the captain's boat had shared a similar fate during the night. Both of these accidents served to arouse us to a still stronger sense of our slender reliance upon the human means at our command and to show us our utter dependence on that divine aid which we so much the more stood in need of.

NOVEMBER 25TH. No change of wind had yet taken place. We experienced the last night the same wet and disagreeable weather of the preceding one.

About eight o'clock in the morning we discovered that the water began to come fast in our boat, and in a few minutes the quantity increased to such a degree as to alarm us considerably for our safety. We commenced immediately a strict search in every part of her to discover the leak, and after tearing up the ceiling or floor of the boat near the bow, we found it proceeded from one of the streaks or outside boards having bursted off there. No time was to be lost in devising some means to repair it. The great difficulty consisted in its being in the bottom of the boat, about six inches from the surface of the water. To enable us to fasten the board on again, it was necessary, therefore, to have access to the outside. The leak being to leeward, we hove about and lay to on the other tack, which brought the side of the boat nearly out of water. The captain, who was at the time ahead of us, seeing us maneuvering to get the boat about, shortened sail, presently tacked, and ran down to us. I informed him of our situation, and he came immediately alongside to our assistance. After directing all the men in the boat to get on one side (the other side, by that means, heeled out of the water a considerable distance), we then managed with a little difficulty to drive in a few nails and to secure it, much beyond our expectations.

Fears of no ordinary kind were excited by this seemingly small accident. When it is recollected to what a slight vessel we had committed ourselves, our means of safety alone consisting in her capacity and endurance for many weeks, in all probability, yet to come, it will not be considered strange that this little accident should not only have damped our spirits considerably but should also have thrown a great gloominess over the natural prospects of our deliverance. On this occasion, too, we were enabled to rescue ourselves from inevitable destruction by the possession of a few nails, without which (had it not been our fortune to save some from the wreck) we would, in all human calculation, have been lost. We were still liable to a recurrence of the same accident, perhaps to a still worse one, as, in the heavy and repeated racking of the swell, the progress of our voyage would serve but to increase the incapacity and weakness of our boat. The starting of a single nail in her bottom would most assuredly prove our certain destruction. We wanted not this additional reflection to add to the miseries of our situation.

NOVEMBER 26TH. Our sufferings, heaven knows, were now sufficiently increased, and we looked forward, not without an extreme dread and anxiety, to the gloomy and disheartening prospect before us. We experienced a little abatement of wind and rough weather today and took the opportunity of drying the bread that had been wet the day previously. To our great joy and satisfaction also, the wind hauled out to east-northeast and enabled us to hold a much more favourable course. With these exceptions, no circumstance of any considerable interest occurred in the course of this day.

The 27th of November was alike undistinguished for any incident worthy of note, except that the wind again veered back to the east and destroyed the fine prospect we had entertained of making a good run for several days to come.

NOVEMBER 28TH. The wind hauled still further to the southward and obliged us to fall off our course to the south. It commenced to blow with such violence as to put us again under short sail.

The night set in extremely dark and tempestuous, and we began to entertain fears that we should be separated. We, however, with great pains, managed to keep about a ship's length apart, so that the white sails of our boats could be distinctly discernible. The captain's boat was but a short distance astern of mine, and that of the second mate a few rods to leeward of his.

At about eleven o'clock at night, having lain down to sleep in the bottom of the boat, I was suddenly awakened by one of my companions, who cried out that the captain was in distress and was calling on us for assistance. I immediately aroused myself and listened a moment, in order to hear if any thing further should be said, when the captain's loud voice arrested my attention. He was calling to the second mate, whose boat was nearer to him than mine. I made all haste to put about, ran down to him, and inquired what was the matter. He replied: "I have been attacked by an unknown fish, and he has stove my boat."

It appeared that some large fish had accompanied the boat for a short distance and had suddenly made an unprovoked attack upon her—as nearly as they could determine—with his jaws. The extreme darkness of the night prevented them from distinguishing what kind of animal it was, but they judged it to be about twelve feet in length and one of the killer-fish species. After having struck the boat once, he continued to play about her on every side, as if manifesting a disposition to renew the attack, and did a second time strike the bow of the boat and split her stem. They had no other instrument of offense but the sprit-pole (a long, slender piece of wood by which the peak of the sail is extended), with which, after the fish's repeated attempts to destroy the boat, they succeeded in beating him off.

I arrived just as he had discontinued his operations and had disappeared. He had made a considerable breach in the bow of the boat, through which the water had begun to pour fast. The captain, imagining matters to be considerably worse than they were, immediately took measures to remove his provisions into the second mate's boat and mine, in order to lighten his own. By that means and by constant bailing, he intended to keep her above water until daylight should enable him to discover the extent of the damage and to repair it.

> ## *"There was a desperate instinct that bound us together."*

The night was spissy darkness itself. The sky was completely overcast, and it seemed to us as if fate was wholly relentless in pursuing us with such a cruel complication of disasters. We were not without our fears that the fish might renew his attack upon one of the other boats sometime during the night and unexpectedly destroy us. But our fears proved entirely groundless, as he was never afterwards seen.

When daylight came, the wind again favoured us a little, and we all lay to to repair the broken boat. This was effected by nailing on thin strips of boards in the inside. Having replaced the provisions in the captain's boat, we proceeded again on our course.

Our allowance of water, which in the commencement merely served to administer to the positive demands of nature, now became insufficient. We began to experience violent thirst from the consumption of the provisions that had been wet with the salt water and dried in the sun. These we were obliged to eat first to prevent their spoiling, and we could not—nay, we did not dare—to make any encroachments on our stock of water. Our determination was to suffer as long as human patience and endurance would hold out, having only in view the relief that would be afforded us when the quantity of wet provisions should be exhausted.

Our extreme sufferings here first commenced. The privation of water is justly ranked among the most dreadful of the miseries of our life. The violence of raving thirst has no parallel in the catalogue of human calamities. It was our hard lot to have felt this in its extremest force, and necessity subsequently compelled us to seek resource from one of the offices of nature. We were not at first aware of the consequences of eating this bread, and it was not until the fatal effects of it had shown themselves to a degree of oppression that we could divine the cause of our extreme thirst. But, alas, there was no relief! Ignorant or instructed of the fact, the bread composed a part of our subsistence, and reason imposed upon us the necessity of its immediate consumption, as otherwise it would have been lost to us entirely.

NOVEMBER 29TH. Our boats appeared to be growing daily more frail and insufficient. The continual flowing of the water into them seemed increased, without our being able to assign it to anything else than a general weakness, arising from causes that must in a short time, without some remedy or relief, produce their total failure. We did not neglect, however, to patch up and mend them, according to our means, whenever we could discover a broken or weak part.

We this day found ourselves surrounded by a shoal of dolphins, some or one of which we tried in vain a long time to take. We made a small line from some rigging that was in the boat, fastened on one of the fish hooks, and tied to it a small piece of white rag. They took not the least notice of it but continued playing around us nearly all day, mocking both our miseries and our efforts.

NOVEMBER 30TH. This was a remarkably fine day. The weather was not exceeded by any that we had experienced since we left the wreck. At one o'clock, I proposed to our boat's crew to kill one of the turtles, two of which we had in our possession. I need not say that the proposition was hailed with the utmost enthusiasm; hunger had set its ravenous gnawings upon our stomachs, and we waited with impatience to suck the warm flowing blood of the animal. A small fire was kindled in the shell of the turtle, and after dividing the blood, of which there was about a gill, among those of us who felt disposed to drink it, we cooked the remainder, entrails and all, and enjoyed from it an unspeakably fine repast. The stomachs of two or three revolted at the sight of the blood, and they refused to partake of it. Not even the outrageous thirst that was upon them could induce them to taste it. For myself, I took it like a medicine to relieve the extreme dryness of my palate and stopped not to inquire whether it was anything else than a liquid. After this, I may say exquisite banquet, our bodies were considerably recruited, and I felt my spirits now much higher than they had been at any time before.

By observation this day, we found ourselves in latitude 7° 53′ south. Our distance from the wreck, as nearly as we could calculate, was then about four hundred and eighty miles.

DECEMBER 1ST. From the 1st to the 3rd of December, exclusive, nothing transpired of any moment. Our boats as yet kept admirably well together, and the weather was distinguished for its mildness and salubrity. We gathered consolation, too, from a favourable slant which the wind took to northeast. Our situation was not at that moment, we thought, so comfortless as we had been led at first to consider it. In our extravagant felicitations upon the blessing of the wind and weather, we forgot our leaks, our weak boats, our own debility, our immense distance from land, and the smallness of our stock of provisions. All of these, when brought to mind with the force which they deserved, were too well calculated to dishearten us and cause us to sigh for the hardships of our lot. Up to the 3rd of December, the raging thirst of our mouths had not been but in a small degree alleviated. Had it not been for the pains which that gave us, we should have tasted, during this spell of fine weather, a species of enjoyment derived from a momentous forgetfulness of our actual situation.

DECEMBER 3RD. With great joy we hailed the last crumb of our damaged bread and commenced this day to take our allowance of healthy provisions. The salutary and agreeable effects of this change were felt at first in so slight a degree as to give us no great cause of comfort or satisfaction. But gradually, as we partook of our small allowance of water, the moisture began to collect in our mouths, and the parching fever of the palate imperceptibly left it.

An accident here happened to us which gave us a great momentary spell of uneasiness. The night was dark and the sky was completely overcast, so that we could scarcely discern each other's boats. At about ten o'clock, that of the second mate was suddenly missing. I felt for a moment considerable alarm at her unexpected disappearance, and after a little reflection I immediately hove to, struck a light as expeditiously as possible, and hoisted it at the masthead in a lantern. Our eyes were now directed over every part of the ocean in search of her when, to our great joy, we discerned an answering light about a quarter of a mile to leeward of us. We ran down to it, and it proved to be the lost boat.

Strange as the extraordinary interest which we felt in each other's company may appear, and much as our repugnance for separation may seem to imply of weakness, it was the subject of our continual hopes and fears. It is truly remarked that misfortune more than anything else serves to endear us to our companions. So strongly was this sentiment engrafted upon our feelings and so closely were the destinies of all of us involuntarily linked together that, had one of the boats been wrecked and wholly lost with all her provisions and water, we should have felt ourselves constrained, by every tie of humanity, to have taken the surviving sufferers into the other boats and to have shared our bread and water with them while a crumb of one or a drop of the other remained.

Hard, indeed, then would the case have been for all, and much as I have since reflected on the subject, I have not been able to realize, had it so happened, that a sense of our necessities would have allowed us to give so magnanimous and devoted a character to our feelings. I can only speak of the impressions which I recollect I had at the time.

Subsequently, however, as our situation became more straitened and desperate, our conversation on this subject took a different turn. It appeared to be a universal sentiment that such a course of conduct was calculated to weaken the chances of a final deliverance for some, and also might be only the means of consigning every soul of us to a horrid death of starvation. There is no question but that an immediate separation, therefore, was the most politic measure that could be adopted and that every boat should take its own separate chance.

While we remained together, should any accident happen of the nature alluded to, only two courses could be adopted: that of taking the survivors into the other boats and thus giving up voluntarily what we were satisfied could alone prolong our hopes and multiply the chances of our safety, or of unconcernedly witnessing their struggles in death, perhaps to beat them from our boats with weapons back into the ocean.

The expectation of reaching the land was founded upon a reasonable calculation of the distance, the means, and the subsistence, which was scanty enough, God knows, and ill adapted to the probable exigencies of the voyage. Any addition to our own demands in this respect would not only injure but also actually destroy the whole system which we had laid down and reduce us to a slight hope, derived either from the speedy death of some of our crew or from the falling in with some vessel.

With all this, however, there was a desperate instinct that bound us together. We could not reason on the subject with any degree of satisfaction to our minds; yet we continued to cling to each other with a strong and involuntary impulse.

This, indeed, was a matter of no small difficulty, and it constituted, more than anything else, a source of continual watching and inquietude. We would but turn our eyes away for a few moments during some dark nights, and presently one of the boats would be missing. There was no other remedy than to heave to immediately and set a light by which the missing boat might be directed to us. These proceedings necessarily interfered very much with our speed and, consequently, lessened our hopes. But we preferred to submit to it while the consequences were not so immediately felt, rather than to part with the consolation which each other's presence afforded.

Nothing of importance took place on the 4th of December.

On the 5th, at night, owing to the extreme darkness and to a strong wind, I again separated from the other boats. Finding they were not to be seen in any direction, I loaded my pistol and fired it twice. Soon after the second discharge they made their appearance a short distance to windward. We joined company and again kept on our course, in which we continued without any remarkable occurrence through the 6th and 7th of December. The wind during this period blew very strong and much more unfavourably. Our boats continued to leak and to take in a good deal of water over the gunwales.

DECEMBER 8TH. In the afternoon of this day, the wind set in east-southeast and began to blow much harder than we had yet experienced it. By twelve o'clock at night it had increased to a perfect gale, with heavy showers of rain. We now began, from these dreadful indications, to prepare ourselves for destruction. We continued to take in sail by degrees, as the tempest gradually increased, until at last we were obliged to take down our masts. At this juncture we gave up entirely to the mercy of the waves.

The sea and rain had wet us to the skin. We sat down silently, awaiting our fate with sullen resignation. We made an effort to catch some fresh water by spreading one of the sails, but after having spent a long time and obtained but a small quantity in a bucket, it proved to be quite as full of salt as that from the ocean. This we attributed to its having passed through the sail, which had been so often wet by the sea and upon which, after drying so frequently in the sun, concretions of salt had been formed. It was a dreadful night—cut off from any imaginary relief. Nothing remained but to wait the approaching issue with firmness and resignation.

The appearance of the heavens was dark and dreary, and the blackness that was spread over the face of the waters was dismal beyond description. The heavy squalls that followed each other in quick succession were preceded by sharp flashes of lightning that appeared to wrap our little barge in flames. The sea rose to a fearful height, and every wave that came looked as if it must be the last that would be necessary for our destruction. To an overruling Providence alone must be attributed our salvation from the horrors of that terrible night. It can be accounted for in no other way that a speck of substance, like that which we were before the driving terrors of the tempest, could have been conducted safely through it.

After twelve o'clock it began to abate a little in intervals of two or three minutes, during which we would venture to raise up our heads and look to windward. Our boat was completely unmanageable. Without sails, mast, or rudder, she had been driven, in the course of the afternoon and night, we knew not whither, nor how far.

When the gale had in some measure subsided, we made efforts to get a little sail upon her and put her head towards the course we had been steering. My companions had not slept any during the whole night and were dispirited and broken down to such a degree as to appear to want some more powerful stimulus than the fear of death to enable them to do their duty. By great exertions, however, towards morning we again set a double-reefed mainsail and jib and began to make tolerable progress on the voyage.

An unaccountable good fortune had kept the boats together during all the troubles of the night. The sun rose and showed the disconsolate faces of our companions once more to each other.

"I proposed to reduce our allowance of provisions one half."

DECEMBER 9TH. By twelve o'clock this day, we were enabled to set all sail as usual, but there continued to be a very
heavy sea running, which opened the seams of the boats and
increased the leaks to an alarming degree. There was, however, no remedy for this but continual bailing, which had
now come to be an extremely irksome and laborious task. By
observation we found ourselves in latitude 17° 40′ south.

At eleven o'clock at night, the captain's boat was unexpectedly found to be missing. After the last accident of this
kind, we had agreed, if the same should again occur, that, in
order to save our time, the other boats should not heave to as
usual but should continue on their course until morning and
thereby save the great detention that must arise from such
repeated delays. We, however, concluded on this occasion to
make a small effort, which, if it did not immediately prove
the means of restoring the lost boat, we would discontinue

and again make sail. Accordingly, we hove to for an hour, during which time I fired my pistol twice, but obtaining no tidings of the boat, we stood on our course. When daylight appeared, she was about two miles to leeward of us. Upon observing her, we immediately ran down and again joined company.

DECEMBER 10TH–17TH. I have omitted to notice the gradual advances which hunger and thirst had made upon us for the last six days. As the time had lengthened since our departure from the wreck and the allowance of provisions shortened, making the demands of the appetite daily more and more importunate, there was created in us an almost uncontrollable temptation to violate our resolution and satisfy, for once, the hard yearnings of nature from our stock. But a little reflection served to convince us of the imprudence and unmanliness of the measure, and it was abandoned with a sort of melancholy effort of satisfaction.

I had taken into custody, by common consent, all the provisions and water belonging to the boat and was determined that no encroachment should be made upon it without my consent. Nay, I felt myself bound by every consideration of duty, by every dictate of sense, prudence, and discretion (without which, in my situation, all the exertions would have been folly itself), to protect them at the hazard of my life. For this purpose I locked up in my chest the whole quantity and never, for a single moment, closed my eyes without placing some part of my person in contact with the chest, and having loaded my pistol, I kept it constantly about me. I should not certainly have put any threats in execution as long as the

American whalemen preparing to take a whale. Their unnamed ship is a typical square-rigged whaler. From a lithograph by the noted American printmaker, Nathaniel Currier. *Forbes Collection, Hart Nautical Museum, M. I. T.*

Captain Owen Chase, former first mate of the *Essex* and author of *Narrative of the Most Extraordinary and Distressing Shipwreck of the Whale-Ship Essex.* From a photograph of a portrait. *Nantucket Historical Association*

PACIFIC

Reca de Plata
Rica de Oro
Lisianskys I.
Necker I.
Bird I.
Montague I.
Cook
Maria Laxara
Morro
Guad...
sebastian Lobos
Desierta
Patrocinio
Krusensterns R.
SANDWICH ISLANDS
Onecheow
Morotoi
la Nublada.
Volcan
Lambas Desierta
Woahoo
Mowee
Ranai
St Bartholomew
Rocks on which the P.r W.m Henry
struck 1796.
Karakakooa
Owhyhee

OCEAN

Artheno
Brown
Ids 1807
Chatham I.s
S.Piedro
Manuel Rodriguez
Cashabas
Patersons I.s
Tibbetson's I.s
Daniels I.s
Palmyras
Land
seen
Bonhams Hope I.s
Elmore
Arrowsmiths I.s
Christmas I.
Mulgraves I.s
Pitt
Matthew's I.
Cookes
Knoys I.
Simpsens I.

Equinoctial Line

Pleasant I.
Halls
3 Isle
Shanks I.
Kingsmill Groupe
Byrons I.
Blaneys
Hope I.
Arthurs I.
L.s Howes Group
S.Augustine
Roberts P.
Henry Martin I.
El Gran Coral
D. of York's I.
Trevennens I.
Rious I.
MARQUESAS
Kennedys I.
Duffs Group
Charlotte
La Spiritu
I. of Clarence
I. of Handsome People
Groningue
Caroline
la Dominica
S.Pedro
E. of Disappointment
La Madelana
Dog I.
Carlshoff
Fink
Wallis's I.
Bernado or
I. of Danger
Flint I.
Tiburones
Horn I.
Oahbooa
Roggeweens I.s
Baumans I.s
The Low IS.
Whytootacke
FRIENDLY ISLANDS
Cocos I.
Palmerston I.
Scilly I.
SOCIETY
Fatti
Maitea
S.Pablo
Thrumcap
Lagoon
S.Narciso
Tacanoowy
Angerara
Boolabola
E. of Wales's
Charlotte I.
Whytootacke
Anamooka
Okatooa
Harvey I.
Otaheite
Bligh Lagoon
Hoggs I.
Tongataboo
Eacowe
Mangea
Wateo
Gloucester I.
S.Telmo
Osnaburg
Gambier I.
Pylstart
Ohetroa I.
Whitsunday I.
Cresent I.
la Incaination
Toobouai High I.
S.Juan Baptista I.
Oparra
The 4 Crowns
E said to be discovered
by the Spaniards in 17?

PACIFIC OCEA

N.C Middletons I.
L. de Vasquez
Norfolk I.
Sunday I.
Rosaretta Reef
Curtis's I.
L.s Howes I.
C.Maria
NEW ZEELAND
Sisters
Chatham I.d
Doubtfull
Saunders
Bounty I.s
Antipodes I.s
Disappointment I.
Lord Aucklands I.s
The Judge
Bishop and Clerk

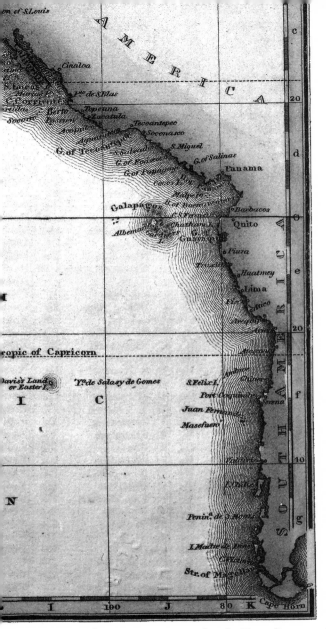

Printed in 1822—two years after the *Essex* disaster—this American-made map of the Pacific shows the Sandwich (Hawaiian) Islands, Easter and Ducie Islands, but not Pitcairn or Henderson Islands.

Morse, J. and S., A New Universal Atlas of the World, New Haven, 1822

TOP: "The *Essex* Struck by a Whale" is the title of this old engraving used, in 1834, to illustrate Captain Pollard's account of the wreck in a collection of sea-disaster stories. BOTTOM: "Discovery of Skeletons" from the same collection, supposedly illustrates Thomas Chapple's account of this gruesome event. But the three well-dressed seamen pictured here scarcely resemble the *Essex* castaways. The Mariner's Chronicle, *New Haven, 1834*

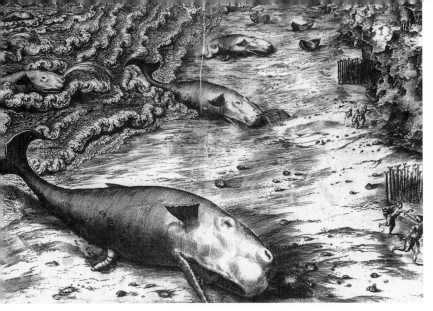

Sperm whales washed up and stranded on the beach. From an early German engraving. *Forbes Collection, Hart Nautical Museum, M. I. T.*

Two harpoons firmly planted in his side, this wounded sperm whale convincingly demonstrates the wild brute fury that characterized his species under attack. From a French lithograph of whaling off the Mexican coast. *Kendall Whaling Museum, Sharon, Massachusetts*

Destruction of a boat from the whaler, *Anne Alexander* of New Bedford. Thirty years after the *Essex* disaster, this ship was also rammed and sunk by a whale. Her crew was rescued two days later. *Forbes Collection, Hart Nautical Museum, M. I. T.*

Capturing giant turtles in the Galápagos Islands. Harper's New Monthly Magazine, *IX* *(August 1859)*

Shipping Paper of the 1817 voyage of the *Essex*, listing the members of her crew, the date each man signed aboard, and his allotted share of the voyage's profits. Note that Captain Pollard was then the *Essex*'s first mate and Owen Chase a boatsteerer or harpooner. *Nantucket Historical Association*

Sperm whale   *Scammon, Charles M.*, The Marine Mammals, *San Francisco, 1874*

North Atlantic right whale   Memoirs of the Boston Society of Natural History, VIII
(September, 1916). *Courtesy of the Boston Museum of Science*

The end of a hard day of whaling. The whalemen are victorious over the
dying sperm whale. A typical scene of the South Pacific. An 1847 print.
Forbes Collection, Hart Nautical Museum, M. I. T.

most distant hopes of reconciliation existed. I had determined, in case the least refractory disposition should be manifested (a thing which I contemplated not unlikely to happen with a set of starving wretches like ourselves), that I would immediately divide our subsistence into equal proportions and give each man's share into his own keeping. Then, should any attempt be made upon mine, which I intended to mete out to myself according to exigencies, I was resolved to make the consequences of it fatal. There was, however, the most upright and obedient behaviour in this respect manifested by every man in the boat, and I never had the least opportunity of proving what my conduct would have been on such an occasion.

While standing on our course this day, we came across a small shoal of flying fish, four of which, in their efforts to avoid us, flew against the mainsail and dropped into the boat. One having fallen near me, I eagerly snatched up and devoured. The other three were immediately taken by the rest and eaten alive. On this occasion, I felt, for the first time, a disposition to laugh, upon witnessing the ludicrous and almost desperate efforts of my five companions, who each sought to get a fish. They were very small of their kind and constituted—scales, wings, and all—but an extremely delicate mouthful for hungry stomachs like ours.

From the 11th to the 13th of December inclusive, our progress was very slow, owing to light winds and calms. Nothing transpired of any moment except that, on the 11th, we killed the only remaining turtle and enjoyed another luxuriant repast, which invigorated our bodies and gave a fresh flow to our spirits. The weather was extremely hot. We were exposed to the full force of a meridian sun, without any covering to shield us from its burning influence or the least breath of air to cool its parching rays.

On the 13th day of December we were blessed with a change of wind to the northward that brought us a most welcome and unlooked for relief. We now, for the first time, actually felt what might be deemed a reasonable hope of our deliverance. With hearts bounding with satisfaction and bosoms swelling with joy, we made all sail to the eastward. We imagined we had run out the trade winds and had got into the variables and should, in all probability, reach the land many days sooner than we expected.

But, alas, our anticipations were but a dream from which we shortly experienced a cruel awaking! The wind gradually died away and at night was succeeded by a perfect calm, which was all the more oppressive and disheartening to us after the bright prospects which had attended us during the day. The gloomy reflections that this hard fortune had given birth to were succeeded by others, of a no less cruel and discouraging nature, when we found the calm continuing during the 14th, 15th, and 16th of December inclusive.

The extreme oppression of the weather, the sudden and unexpected prostration of our hopes, and the consequent dejection of our spirits set us again to thinking and filled our souls with fearful and melancholy forebodings. In this state of affairs, seeing no alternative left us but to employ to the best advantage all human expedients in our power, I proposed, on the 14th, to reduce our allowance of provisions one-half. No objections were made to this arrangement; all submitted, or seemed to do so, with an admirable fortitude and forbearance.

The proportion which our stock of water bore to our bread was not large, and while the weather continued so oppressive, we did not think it advisable to diminish our scanty pittance. Indeed, it would have been scarcely possible to have done so, with any regard for our necessities. Our thirst had become now incessantly more intolerable than hunger, and the quantity then allowed was barely sufficient to keep the mouth in a state of moisture for about one-third of the time. "Patience and long-suffering" was the constant language of our lips. Strong as the resolves of the soul could make it, we determined to cling to existence as long as hope and breath remained to us.

In vain was every expedient tried to relieve the raging fever of the throat by drinking salt water and by holding small quantities of it in the mouth. By that means, the thirst was increased to such a degree as even to drive us to despairing—and vain—relief from our own urine.

Our sufferings during these calm days almost exceeded human belief. The hot rays of the sun beat down upon us to such a degree as to oblige us to hang over the gunwale of the boat into the sea to cool our weak and fainting bodies. This expedient afforded us, however, a grateful relief and was productive of a discovery of infinite importance to us. No sooner had one of us got on the outside of the gunwale than he immediately observed the bottom of the boat to be covered with a species of small clam, which, upon being tasted, proved a most delicious and agreeable food. This was no sooner announced to us than we commenced to tear them off and to eat them for a few minutes like a set of gluttons.

After having satisfied the immediate craving of the stomach, we gathered large quantities and laid them up in the boat, but hunger came upon us again in less than half an hour afterwards, within which time they had all disappeared. Upon attempting to get into the sea again, we found ourselves so weak as to require each other's assistance. Indeed, had it not been for three of our crew, who could not swim and who did not, therefore, get overboard, I know not by what means we should have been able to have resumed our situations in the boat.

On the 15th our boat continued to take in water so fast from her leaks, and the weather proving so moderate, we concluded to search out the bad places and to endeavour to mend them as well as we should be able. After a considerable search and after removing the ceiling near the bows, we found the principal opening was occasioned by the starting of a plank or streak in the bottom of the boat next to the keel. To remedy this, it was now absolutely necessary to have access to the bottom, though the means of doing so did not immediately occur to our minds. After a moment's reflection, however, one of the crew, Benjamin Lawrence, offered to tie a rope around his body, take a boat's hatchet in his hand, and thus go under the water. He proposed to hold the hatchet against a nail—to be driven through from the inside—for the purpose of clenching it. This was, accordingly, all effected with some little trouble and answered the purpose much beyond our expectations.

Our latitude was this day, the 15th, 21° 42′ south. The oppression of the weather, still continuing through the 16th, bore upon our health and spirits with an amazing force and severity. The most disagreeable excitements were produced by it, which, added to the disconsolate endurance of the calm, called loudly for some mitigating expedient—some sort of relief to our prolonged sufferings. By our observations on that day, we found, in addition to our other calamities, that we had been urged back from our progress, by the heave of the sea, a distance of ten miles—and we were still without any prospect of wind.

In this distressing posture of our affairs, the captain proposed that we should commence rowing, which, being seconded by all, we immediately concluded to take a double allowance of provisions and water for the day and to row during the cool of the nights, until we should get a breeze from some quarter or other. Accordingly, when night came, we commenced our labourious operations.

We made but a very sorry progress. Hunger and thirst and long inactivity had so weakened us that, in three hours, every man gave out, and we abandoned the further prosecution of the plan. With the sunrise the next morning, on the 17th, a light breeze sprung up from the southeast, and although directly ahead, it was welcomed with almost frenzied feelings of gratitude and joy.

DECEMBER 18TH. The wind had increased this day considerably. By twelve o'clock it blew a gale, veering from southeast to east-southeast. Again we were compelled to take in all sail and lie to for the principal part of the day. At night, however, the gale died away. The next day, the 19th, proved very moderate and pleasant weather, and we again commenced to make a little progress.

"There is land!"

DECEMBER 20TH. This was a day of great happiness and joy. After having experienced one of the most distressing nights in the whole catalogue of our sufferings, we awoke to a morning of comparative luxury and pleasure.

About seven o'clock, while we were sitting dispirited, silent, and dejected in our boats, one of our companions suddenly and loudly called out: "There is land!"

We were all aroused in an instant, as if electrified. We cast our eyes to leeward, and there, indeed, was the blessed vision before us, "as plain and palpable" as could be wished for.

A new and extraordinary impulse now took possession of us. We shook off the lethargy of our senses and seemed to take on another and fresh existence. One or two of my companions—whose lagging spirits and worn-out frames had begun to inspire them with an utter indifference to their fate—now immediately brightened up and manifested a surprising alacrity and earnestness to gain, without delay, the much wished for shore.

It appeared at first a low white beach and lay like a basking paradise before our longing eyes. It was discovered nearly at the same time by the other boats, and a general burst of joy and congratulation now passed between us. To divine what the feelings of our hearts were on this occasion is not within the scope of human calculation. Alternate expectation, fear, gratitude, surprise, and exultation swayed our minds and quickened our exertions.

We ran down for the beach, and at eleven o'clock, A.M., we were within a quarter of a mile of the shore.

It was an island, to all appearance, about six miles long and three broad, with a very high, rugged shore, and surrounded by rocks. The sides of the mountains were bare, but the tops of them looked fresh and green with vegetation. Upon examining our navigators, we found it was Ducie Island, lying in latitude 24° 40′ south, longitude 124° 40′ west.

A short moment sufficed for reflection, and we then made immediate arrangements to land. None of us knew whether the island was inhabited or not, nor what it afforded, if anything. If inhabited, it was uncertain whether by beasts or by savages, and a momentary suspense was created by contemplation of the dangers which might possibly arise by proceeding without due preparation and care. Hunger and thirst, however, soon determined us, and having taken the musket and pistols, I, with three others, effected a landing upon some sunken rocks and waded thence to the shore. Upon arriving at the beach, it was necessary to take a little breath and to lie down for a few minutes to rest our weak bodies before we could proceed.

Let the reader judge, if he can, what must have been our feelings now and he will have but a faint idea of the happiness that here fell to our lot! After being bereft of all comfortable hopes of life for the space of thirty days of terrible suffering—with our bodies wasted to mere skeletons by hunger and thirst and with death itself staring us in the face—we were suddenly and unexpectedly conducted to a rich banquet of food and drink, which subsequently we enjoyed for a few days to our full satisfaction.

We now, after a few minutes, separated and went in different directions in search of water, the want of which had been our principal privation and called for immediate relief. I had not proceeded far in my excursion before I discovered a fish, about a foot and a half in length, swimming along in the water close to the shore. I commenced an attack upon him with the breach of my gun and struck him, I believe, once. He ran under a small rock that lay near the shore. From there I took him with the aid of my ramrod. I brought him on the beach and immediately fell to eating him. My companions soon joined in the repast, and in less than ten minutes the whole was consumed—bones, skin, scales, and all.

With full stomachs, we imagined we could now attempt the mountains, where we considered water—if on any part of the island—would be most probably obtained. I accordingly clambered with excessive labour, suffering, and pain up amongst the bushes, roots, and underwood of one of the crags, looking as I went in all directions in vain for every appearance of water that might present itself. There was no indication of the least moisture to be found within the distance to which I had ascended—although my strength did not enable me to get higher than about twenty feet. I was sitting down at the height that I had attained to gather a little breath, and was ruminating there upon the fruitlessness of my search and on the consequent evils and continuation of suffering that it necessarily implied, when I perceived that the tide had risen considerably since our landing. It threatened to cut off our retreat to the rocks—by which alone we should be able to regain our boats. I therefore determined to proceed again to the shore to inform the captain and the rest of our want of success in procuring water and to consult upon the propriety of remaining at the island any longer.

I never for one moment lost sight of the main chance, which I conceived we still had, of either getting to the coast or of meeting with some vessel at sea. And I felt that every minute's detention, without some equivalent purpose, was lessening those chances by a consumption of the means of our support.

When I had got down, one of my companions informed me that he had found a place, in a rock some distance off, from which the water exuded in small drops at intervals of about five minutes. He had, by applying his lips to the rock, obtained a few of these drops, which only served to whet his appetite and from which nothing like the least satisfaction had proceeded. Upon this information, I immediately resolved in my own mind to advise remaining until morning in order to endeavour to make a more thorough search the next day, as well as to pick away the rock, which had been discovered, with our hatchets—with the view of increasing, if possible, the run of the water.

We all repaired again to our boats. There we found that the captain had the same impressions as to the propriety of our delay until morning. We therefore landed and, having hauled our boats up on the beach, lay down in them that night. Free from all the anxieties of watching and labour, we gave ourselves up, amid our sufferings of hunger and thirst, to an unreserved forgetfulness and peace of mind that seemed so well to accord with the pleasing anticipations that this day had brought forth.

It was but a short space, however, until the morning broke upon us. Sense and feeling, gnawing hunger, and the raging fever of thirst then made me redouble my wishes and efforts to explore the island again. By traversing the shore a considerable distance that night, we had obtained a few crabs and a few very small fish. But we waited until the next day to begin the labours for which we considered a night of refreshing and undisturbed repose would better qualify us.

DECEMBER 21ST. We had still reserved our common allowance, but it was entirely inadequate for the purpose of supplying the raging demands of the palate. Such an excessive and cruel thirst was created as almost to deprive us of the power of speech. The lips became cracked and swollen, and a sort of glutinous saliva, disagreeable to the taste and intolerable beyond expression, collected in the mouth. Our bodies had wasted away to almost skin and bone and possessed so little strength as often to require each other's assistance in performing some of its weakest functions. Relief, we now felt, must come soon, or nature would sink. The most perfect discipline was still maintained in respect to our provisions, and it now became our whole object—if we should not be able to replenish our subsistence from the island—to obtain, by some other means or other, a sufficient refreshment to enable us to prosecute our voyage.

Our search for water, accordingly, again commenced with the morning; each of us took a different direction and prosecuted the examination of every place where there was the least indication of it. The small leaves of the shrubbery afforded a temporary alleviation by being chewed in the mouth and, but for the peculiarly bitter taste which those of the island possessed, would have been an extremely grateful substitute. In the course of our rambles, too, we would now and then meet with tropic birds of a beautiful figure and plumage. These occupied small holes in the sides of the mountain, from whence we plucked them without the least difficulty. Upon our approaching them, they made no attempts to fly, nor did they appear to notice us at all. These birds served as for a fine repast. Numbers of them were caught in the course of the day, cooked by fires which we made on the shore, and eaten with the utmost avidity.

We found also a plant, in taste not unlike the peppergrass, growing in considerable abundance in the crevices of the rocks, which proved to us a very agreeable food when chewed with the meat of the birds. These, with a few birds' nests—some of them full of young, others of eggs—which we found in the course of the day, served us for food and supplied the place of our bread. During our stay here, we had restricted ourselves from the use of this provision.

But water, the great object of all our anxieties and exertions, was nowhere to be found, and we began to despair of meeting with it on the island. Our state of extreme weakness—and many of us were without shoes or any covering for the feet—prevented us from exploring any great distance, lest, by some sudden faintness or overexertion, we should not be able to return and at night be exposed to attacks of wild beasts, which might inhabit the island. Beyond the reach of the feeble assistance that otherwise could be afforded to each, we were alike incapable of resistance.

The whole day was thus consumed in picking up whatever had the least shape or quality of sustenance. Before us was another night of misery, which was to be passed without a drop of water to cool our parching tongues. In this state of affairs, we would not reconcile it to ourselves to remain longer at this place. A day, an hour lost to us unnecessarily here might cost us our preservation. A drop of the water that we then had in our possession might prove, in the last stages of our debility, the very cordial of life.

I addressed the substance of these few reflections to the captain, who agreed with me upon the necessity of taking some decisive steps in our present dilemma. After some considerable conversation on this subject, it was finally concluded to spend the succeeding day in the further search for water and, if none should be found, to quit the island the morning after.

DECEMBER 22ND. We had been employed during the last night in various occupations, according to the feelings or the wants of the men. Some continued to wander about the shore and to short distances in the mountains, still seeking for food and water. Others hung about the beach, near the edge of the sea, endeavouring to take the little fish that came about them. Some slept, insensible to every feeling but rest, while others spent the night in talking of their situation and reasoning upon the probabilities of their deliverance. The dawn of day aroused us again to labour, and each of us pursued his own inclination as to the course taken over the island after water.

My principal hope was founded upon my success in picking the rocks where the moisture had been discovered two days before, and thither I hastened as soon as my strength would enable me to get there. It was about a quarter of a mile from what I may call our encampment. With two men, who had accompanied me, I commenced my labours with a hatchet and an old chisel.

The rock proved to be very soft, and in a very short time I had obtained a considerable hole, but, alas, without the least wished for effect! I watched it for some little time with great anxiety, hoping that, as I increased the depth of the hole, the water would presently flow, but all my hopes and efforts were unavailing. At last I desisted from further labour and sat down near the rock in utter despair.

As I turned my eyes towards the beach, I saw some of the men in the act of carrying a keg along from the boats with, I thought, an extraordinary spirit and activity. The idea suddenly darted across my mind that they had found water and were taking a keg to fill it. I quitted my seat in a moment and made my way towards them with a palpitating heart. Before I came up with them, they gave me the cheering news that they had found a spring of water. I felt, at that moment, as if I could have fallen down and thanked God for this signal act of His mercy. The sensation that I experienced was indeed strange and such as I shall never forget. At one instant I felt an almost choking excess of joy, and at the next I wanted the relief of a flood of tears.

When I arrived at the spot, whither I had hastened as fast

as my weak legs would carry me, I found my companions had all taken their fill. With an extreme degree of forbearance, I then satisfied myself by drinking in small quantities and at intervals of two or three minutes apart. Notwithstanding the remonstrances of prudence and, in some cases, force, many of the men had lain down and thoughtlessly swallowed large quantities of it, until they could drink no more. The effect of this was, however, neither so sudden nor bad as we had imagined. It only served to make them a little stupid and indolent for the remainder of the day.

*"I hastily bid them good-bye,
hoped they would do well,
and came away."*

Upon examining the place from whence we had obtained this miraculous and unexpected succour, we were equally astonished and delighted with the discovery. It was on the shore; above it the sea flowed to the depth of nearly six feet at high tide, and we could procure the water, therefore, from it only when the tide was down. The crevice from which the spring rose was in a flat rock. We filled our two kegs before the tide rose and went back again to our boats. The remainder of this day was spent in seeking for fish, crabs, birds, and anything else that fell in our way that could contribute to satisfy our appetites.

We enjoyed, during that night, a most comfortable and delicious sleep, unattended with those violent cravings of hunger and thirst that had poisoned our slumbers for so many previous ones. Since the discovery of the water, too, we began to entertain different notions altogether of our situation. There was no doubt we might here depend upon a constant and ample supply of it as long as we chose to remain. And in all probability, we could manage to obtain food until the island should be visited by some vessel or until time allowed us to devise other means of leaving it. Our boats would still remain to us, and a stay here might enable us to mend, strengthen, and put them in more perfect order for the sea and get ourselves so far recruited as to be able to endure, if necessary, a more protracted voyage to the mainland.

I made a silent determination in my own mind that I would myself pursue something like this plan, whatever might be the opinion of the rest, but I found no difference in the views of any of us as to this matter. We therefore concluded to remain at least four or five days. Within this time, it could be sufficiently known whether it would be advisable to make any arrangements for a more permanent abode.

DECEMBER 23RD. At eleven o'clock, A.M., we again visited our spring. The tide had fallen to about a foot below it, and we were able to procure, before it rose again, about twenty gallons of water. It was at first a little brackish but soon became fresh from the constant supply from the rock and the departure of the sea. Our observations this morning tended to give us every confidence in its quantity and quality. We therefore rested perfectly easy in our minds on the subject and commenced to make further discoveries about the island.

Each man sought for his own daily living on whatsoever the mountains, the shore, or the sea could furnish him with. Every day during our stay there, the whole time was employed in roving about for food. We found, however, on the 24th, that we had picked up everything that could be got at in the way of sustenance. And, much to our surprise, some of the men came in at night and complained of not having gotten sufficient during the day to satisfy the cravings of their stomachs. Every accessible part of the mountain contiguous to us—or within the reach of our weak enterprise—was already ransacked for birds' eggs and grass and was rifled of all that it contained, so we began to entertain serious apprehensions that we should not be able to live long here. With the view of being prepared as well as possible, should necessity at any time oblige us to quit the island, we commenced, on the 24th, to repair our boats.

We continued to work upon them all that and the succeeding day. We were enabled to do this with much facility by drawing them up and turning them over on the beach, working by spells of two or three hours at a time and then leaving off to seek for food.

We procured our water daily when the tide would leave the shore, but on the evening of the 25th, we found that a fruitless search for nourishment had not repaid us for the labours of a whole day. There was no one thing on the island upon which we could in the least degree rely except the peppergrass. The supply of that was precarious, and it was not much relished without some other food. Our situation here, therefore, now became worse than it would have been in our boats on the ocean. In the latter case, we should be still making some progress towards the land while our provisions lasted, and, too, the chance of falling in with some vessel would be considerably increased. It was certain that we ought not to remain here unless we felt the strongest assurances in our own minds of sufficient sustenance, in regular supplies, that might be depended upon.

After much conversation amongst us on the subject and after again examining our navigators, it was finally concluded to set sail for Easter Island, which we found to be east-southeast from us in latitude 27° 9′ south, longitude 109° 35′ west. All we knew of this island was that it existed as laid down in the books. Of its extent, productions, or inhabitants, if any, we were entirely ignorant. At any rate, it was nearer by eight hundred and fifty miles to the coast and could not be worse in its productions than the one we were about to leave.

The 26th of December was wholly employed in preparations for our departure. Our boats were hauled down to the vicinity of the spring, and our casks—and everything else that would contain water—filled with it.

There had been considerable talk between three of our companions about their remaining on this island and taking their chance both for a living on it and an escape from it. As the time at which we were to leave drew near, they made up their minds to stay behind. The rest of us could make no objection to their plan as it lessened the load of our boats and allowed us their share of the provisions. Moreover, the probability of their being able to sustain themselves on the island (being few in number) was much stronger than that of our reaching the mainland. Should we, however, ever arrive safely, it would become our duty, and we so assured them, to give information of their situation and to make every effort to procure their removal from the island.

Their names were William Wright of Barnstable, Massachusetts, Thomas Chapple of Plymouth, England, and Seth

Weeks of the former place. They had begun, before we came away, to construct a sort of habitation, composed of the branches of trees. We left with them every little article that could be spared from the boats. It was their intention to build a considerable dwelling, which would protect them from the rains, as soon as time and materials could be provided.

The captain wrote letters, which were to be left on the island. These gave information as to the fate of the ship and of ourselves and stated that we had set out to reach Easter Island. Further details were added in an attempt to give notice of our misfortunes should our three fellow sufferers die there and the place afterwards ever be visited by any vessel. These letters were put in a tin case, which was enclosed in a small wooden box and nailed to a tree on the west side of the island near our landing place. We had observed, some days previously, the name of a ship, the *Elizabeth*, cut out in the bark of this tree, which rendered it indubitable that a vessel of that name had once touched here. There was, however, no date to it, nor anything else by which any further particulars could be made out.

DECEMBER 27TH. I went, before we set sail this morning, and procured for each boat a flat stone and two armfuls of wood, with which to make a fire in our boats, should it afterwards become necessary in the further prosecution of our voyage. We calculated we might catch a fish or a bird, and, in that case, we would be provided with the means of cooking it. Otherwise, we knew, from the intense heat of the weather, that they could not be preserved from spoiling.

By ten o'clock, A.M., the tide had risen far enough to allow our boats to float over the rocks. We made all sail and steered around the island for the purpose of making a little further observation. This would not detain us any great time and might be productive of some unexpected good fortune.

Before we started, we missed our three companions and found they had not come down, either to assist us to get off or to take any kind of leave of us. I walked up the beach towards their rude dwelling and informed them that we were then about to set sail and should probably never see them more. They seemed to be very much affected, and one of them shed tears. They wished us to write to their relations, should Providence safely direct us again to our homes, but said little else. They had every confidence in being able to procure a subsistence there as long as they remained. Finding them ill at heart about taking any leave of us, I hastily bid them good-bye, hoped they would do well, and came away. They followed me with their eyes until I was out of sight, and I never saw more of them.

On the northwest side of the island we perceived a fine white beach, on which we imagined we might land and, in a short time, ascertain if any further useful discoveries could be effected or if any addition could be made to our stock of provisions. Having set ashore five or six of the men for this purpose, the rest of us shoved off the boats and commenced fishing. We saw a number of sharks, but all efforts to take them proved ineffectual, and we got but a few small fish, about the size of mackerel, which we divided amongst us. In this business we were occupied until six o'clock in the afternoon, when the men returned to the shore from their search in the mountains. They brought with them a few birds.

We again set sail and steered directly for Easter Island. During that night—after we had got quite clear of the land—

we had a fine strong breeze from the northwest. We kept our fires going, cooked our fish and birds, and felt our situation as comfortable as could be expected. We continued on our course, consuming our provisions and water as sparingly as possible, without any material incident until the 30th of December, when the wind hauled on east-southeast directly ahead. It so continued until the 31st, when it again came to the northward, and we resumed our course.

On the 3rd of January we experienced heavy squalls from the west-southwest, accompanied with dreadful thunder and lightning that threw a gloomy and cheerless aspect over the ocean and incited a recurrence of some of those heavy and desponding moments that we had before experienced. We commenced from Ducie Island to keep a regular reckoning, by which, on the 4th of January, we found we had got to the southward of Easter Island. With the wind prevailing east-northeast, we should not be able to get on to the eastward so as to reach it.

Our birds and fish were all now consumed, and we had begun again upon our short allowance of bread. It was necessary in this state of things to change our determination of going to Easter Island and to shape our course in some other direction where the wind would allow of our going. We had but little hesitation in concluding, therefore, to steer for the Juan Fernández Islands, which lay east-southeast from us some two thousand five hundred miles. We bent our course accordingly towards them.

For the two succeeding days we had very light winds and suffered excessively from the intense heat of the sun. The 7th of January brought us a change of wind to the northward, and at twelve o'clock we found ourselves in latitude 30° 18′

south, longitude 117° 29' west. We continued to make what progress we could to the eastward.

JANUARY 10TH. Matthew P. Joy, the second mate, had suffered debility from the privations we had experienced, much beyond any of the rest of us. On the 8th, he was removed to the captain's boat, under the impression that he would be more comfortable there and that more attention and pains could be bestowed in nursing and endeavouring to comfort him. This day being calm, he manifested a desire to be taken back again. But at four o'clock in the afternoon—having been, according to his wishes, placed in his own boat—he died very suddenly after his removal.

On the 11th, at six o'clock in the morning, we sewed him up in his clothes, tied a large stone to his feet, and having brought all the boats to, consigned him in a solemn manner to the ocean.

This man did not die of absolute starvation, although his end was no doubt very much hastened by his sufferings. He had a weak and sickly constitution and had complained of being unwell the whole voyage. It was an incident, however, which threw a gloom over our feelings for many days. In consequence of his death, one man from the captain's boat was placed in the boat from which he died to supply his place. We then stood away again on our course.

On the 12th of January we had the wind from the northwest, which commenced in the morning and came on to blow before night a perfect gale. We were obliged to take in all sail and to run before the wind. Flashes of lightning were quick and vivid, and the rain came down in cataracts. As, however, the gale blew us fairly on our course and as our speed had been great during the day, we derived, I may say, even pleasure from the uncomfortableness and fury of the storm. But we were apprehensive that, in the darkness of this night, we should be separated and made arrangements for each boat to keep to an east-southeast course all night.

About eleven o'clock—my boat being ahead a short distance of the others—I turned my head back, as I was in the habit of doing every minute, and neither of the others was to be seen. It was blowing and raining at this time as if the heavens were separating, and I knew not hardly at the moment what to do. I hove my boat to the wind and lay drifting about an hour, expecting every moment that they would come up with me. Not seeing anything of them, I put away again and stood on the course agreed upon, with strong hopes that daylight would enable me to discover them again.

When the morning dawned, in vain did we look over every part of the ocean for our companions. They were gone! And we saw no more of them afterwards. By my observation we separated in latitude 32° 16′ south, longitude 112° 20′ west.

"The terrible noise of the whale spouts near us sounded in our ears."

It was folly to repine at the circumstance. It could neither be remedied, nor could sorrow secure their return. But it was impossible to prevent ourselves from feeling all the poignancy and bitterness that characterizes the separation of men who have long suffered in each other's company and whose interests and feelings fate had so closely linked together.

For many days after this accident, our progress was attended with dull and melancholy reflections. We had lost the cheering of each other's faces, which, strange as it is, we so much required in both our mental and bodily distresses.

The 14th of January proved another very squally and rainy day. We had now been nineteen days from the island and had only made a distance of about nine hundred miles. Necessity began to whisper to us that a still further reduction of our allowance must take place or else we must abandon altogether the hopes of reaching the land and rely wholly on the chance of being taken up by a vessel.

How to reduce the daily quantity of food with any regard for life itself was a question of the utmost consequence. Upon our first leaving the wreck, the demands of the stomach had been circumscribed to the smallest possible measure. Subsequently, before reaching the island, there had been a diminution in this already pitiable ration of nearly one half, and it was now, from a reasonable calculation, necessary to curtail even that at least one half again, which must, in a short time, reduce us to mere skeletons again.

We had a full allowance of water, but it only served to contribute to our debility, as our bodies derived only the scanty support which an ounce and a half of bread for each man afforded. It required a great effort to bring matters to this dreadful alternative: either to feed our bodies—and our hopes—a little longer or, in the agonies of hunger, to seize upon and devour our provisions and then coolly to await the approach of death.

We were as yet just able to move about in our boat and to slowly perform the necessary labours appertaining to her. But we were fast wasting away with the relaxing effects of the water, and we daily almost perished under the torrid rays of a meridian sun, to escape from which, we would lie down in the bottom of the boat, cover ourselves over with the sails, and abandon her to the mercy of the waves. Upon attempting to rise again, the blood would rush into the head, and an intoxicating blindness would come over us—almost to occasion our suddenly falling down again. A slight interest was still kept up in our minds by the distant hopes of yet meeting with the other boats, but it was never realized.

An accident occurred at night, which gave me a great cause of uneasiness and led me to an unpleasant rumination upon the probable consequences of a repetition of it. I had lain down in the boat without taking the usual precaution of securing the lid of the provision chest, as I was accustomed to do, when one of the men awoke me and informed me that one of his companions had taken some bread from it.

I felt at the moment the highest indignation and resentment at such conduct in any of our crew. I immediately took my pistol in my hand and charged the man, if he had taken bread, to give it up without the least hesitation or I should instantly shoot him! He became at once very much alarmed and, trembling, confessed the fact, pleading the hard necessity that urged him to it. He appeared to be very penitent for his crime and earnestly swore that he would never be guilty of it again. I could not find it in my soul to extend towards him the least severity on this account, however much, according to the strict imposition which we felt upon ourselves, it might demand. This was the first infraction; and the security of our lives and our hopes of redemption from our sufferings loudly called for a prompt and signal punishment, but every humane feeling of nature plead in his behalf. He was permitted to escape with the solemn injunction that a repetition of the same offense would cost him his life.

I had almost determined upon this occurrence to divide our provisions and to give to each man his share of the whole stock. I should have done so in the height of my resentment had it not been for the reflection that some might, by imprudence, be tempted to go beyond the daily allowance, or to consume it all at once and bring on a premature weakness or starvation. This would of course disable them for the duties of the boat and reduce our chances of safety and deliverance.

On the 15th of January, at night, a very large shark was observed swimming about us in a most ravenous manner. He made attempts every now and then upon different parts of the boat, as if he would devour the very wood with hunger. Several times he came and snapped at the steering oar and even at the sternpost. We tried in vain to stab him with a lance, but we were so weak as to be unable to make any impression upon his hard skin. He was so much larger than an ordinary shark and manifested such a fearless malignity as to make us afraid of him. Our utmost efforts, which were at first directed to kill him for prey, became in the end self-defense. Baffled, however, in all his hungry attempts upon us, he shortly made off.

On the 16th of January, we were surrounded with porpoises in great numbers that followed us nearly an hour and also defied all maneuvers to catch them. The 17th and 18th proved to be calm, but the distresses of a cheerless prospect and a burning hot sun were again visited upon our accursed heads.

We began to think that Divine Providence had abandoned us at last, and it was but an unavailing effort to endeavour to further prolong a now tedious existence. Horrible were the feelings that took possession of us! The contemplation of a death of agony and torment, heightened by the most dreadful and distressing reflections, absolutely prostrated both body and soul. There was not a hope now remaining to us save that which was derived from a sense of the mercies of our Creator.

The night of January 18th was a despairing time in our

sufferings. Our minds were wrought up to the highest pitch of dread and apprehension for our fate, and in them all was dark, gloomy, and confused. About eight o'clock, the terrible noise of whale spouts near us sounded in our ears. We could distinctly hear the furious thrashing of their tails in the water, and our weak minds pictured their appalling and hideous aspects. One of my companions, a black man, took an immediate fright and solicited me to take out the oars and to endeavour to get away from them. I consented to his using any means for that purpose, but, alas, it was wholly out of our power to raise a single arm in our own defense. Two or three of the whales came down near us and went swiftly off across our stern, blowing and spouting at a terrible rate; however, after an hour or two they disappeared, and we saw no more of them.

The next day, the 19th of January, we had extremely bois-terous weather, with rain, heavy thunder, and lightning, which reduced us again to the necessity of taking in all sail and lying to. The wind blew from every point of the compass within the twenty-four hours and, at last, towards the next morning settled at east-northeast—a strong breeze.

JANUARY 20TH. The black man, Richard Peterson, mani-fested today symptoms of a speedy dissolution. For the last three days he had been lying, utterly dispirited and broken down, between the seats in the boat, without being able to do the least duty or hardly to place his hand to his head. This morning he had made up his mind to die rather than to en-dure further misery. He refused his allowance of bread, said he was sensible of his approaching end and was perfectly ready to die. In a few minutes he became speechless. The breath appeared to be leaving his body without producing the least pain. At four o'clock he was gone.

I had, two days previously, conversations with him on the subject of religion, on which he reasoned very sensibly and with much composure. He begged me to let his wife know his fate if ever I reached home in safety. The next morning we committed him to the sea, in latitude 35° 07' south, longitude 105° 46' west.

The wind prevailed to the eastward until the 24th of January, when it again fell calm. We were now in a most wretched and sinking state of debility, hardly able to crawl around the boat and possessing but strength enough to convey our scanty morsel to our mouths. When I perceived this morning that it was calm, my fortitude almost forsook me. I thought to suffer another scorching day like the last we had experienced would close before night the scene of our miseries. I felt many a despairing moment that day that had well nigh proved fatal. It required an effort beyond what I felt I was capable of making to look calmly forward and to contemplate what was yet in store for us. What it was that buoyed me above all the terrors which surrounded us, God alone knows.

Our ounce and a half of bread, which was to serve us all day, was in some cases greedily devoured, as if life was to continue but another moment. At other times, it was hoarded up and eaten crumb by crumb, at regular intervals during the day, as if it was to last us forever. To add to our calamities, boils began to break out upon us, and our imaginations shortly became as diseased as our bodies.

I lay down at night to catch a few moments of oblivious sleep, and immediately my starving fancy was at work. I dreamt of being placed near a splendid and rich repast, where there was everything that the most finicky appetite could desire, and I contemplated the moment in which we were to commence to eat with enraptured feelings of delight. Just as I was about to partake of it, I suddenly awoke to the cold realities of my miserable situation. Nothing could have oppressed me so much. It set such a longing frenzy for victuals in my mind that I felt as if I could have wished the dream to continue forever, as if I never might have awoke from it. I cast a sort of vacant stare about the boat until my eyes rested upon a bit of tough cowhide, which was fastened to one of the oars. I eagerly seized it and commenced to chew it, but there was no substance in it, and it only served to fatigue my weak jaws and add to my bodily pains.

My fellow sufferers murmured very much the whole time and continued to press me continually with questions upon the probability of our reaching land again. I kept constantly rallying my spirits to enable me to afford them comfort. I encouraged them to bear up against all evils and—if we must perish—to die in our own cause and not weakly distrust the providence of the Almighty by giving ourselves up to despair. I reasoned with them and told them that we would not die sooner by keeping up our hopes and that the dreadful sacrifices and privations we endured were to preserve us from death. These were not to be put in competition with the price which we set upon our lives, or with their value to our families. It was, besides, unmanly to repine at what neither admitted of alleviation nor cure. Withal, it was our solemn duty to recognize in our calamities an overruling Divinity, by Whose mercy we might be suddenly snatched from peril. We must rely upon Him alone "Who tempers the wind to the shorn lamb."

"It was without any objection agreed to."

The three following days, the 25th, 26th, and 27th, were not distinguished by any particular circumstances. The wind still prevailed to the eastward and, by its obduracy, almost tore the very hopes of our hearts away. It was impossible to silence the rebellious repinings of our nature at witnessing such a succession of hard fortune against us. It was our cruel lot not to have had one bright anticipation realized— nor one wish of our thirsting souls gratified. We had, at the end of these three days, been urged to the southward as far as latitude 36′, into a chilly region where rains and squalls prevailed. We now calculated to tack and stand back to the northward. After much labour, we got our boat about, and so great was the fatigue attending this small exertion of our bodies that we all gave up for a moment and abandoned her to her own course. Not one of us had now strength sufficient to steer or, indeed, to make one single effort towards getting the sails properly trimmed to enable us to make any headway. After an hour or two of rest, during which the horrors of our situation came upon us with a despairing force and effect, we made a sudden effort and got our sails into such a disposition that the boat would steer herself. We then threw ourselves down, awaiting the issue of time to bring us relief or to take us from the scene of our troubles. We could now do nothing more. Strength and spirits were totally gone. What indeed could have been the narrow hopes that in our situation then bound us to life?

JANUARY 28TH. Our spirits this morning were hardly sufficient to allow of our enjoying a change of the wind, which took place to the westward. It had nearly become indifferent to us from what quarter it blew. Nothing but the slight chance of meeting with a vessel remained to us now. It was this narrow comfort alone that prevented me from lying down at once to die. Only fourteen days' stinted allowance of provisions remained. It was absolutely necessary, however, to increase the quantity of it to enable us to live five days longer. We therefore partook of it as pinching necessity demanded and gave ourselves wholly up to the guidance and disposal of our Creator.

During the 29th and 30th of January the wind continued west, and we made considerable progress until the 31st, when it again came from ahead and prostrated all our hopes. On the 1st of February it changed again to the westward and on the 2nd and 3rd blew to the eastward. It was light and variable until the 8th of February.

Our sufferings were now drawing to a close. A terrible death appeared shortly to await us. Hunger became violent and outrageous, and we prepared for a speedy release from our troubles. Our speech and reason were both considerably impaired, and we were reduced at this time to being certainly the most helpless and wretched of the whole human race.

Isaac Cole, one of our crew, had the day before this, in a fit of despair, thrown himself down in the boat, determined to calmly wait there for death. It was obvious that he had no chance. All was dark, he said, in his mind. Not a single ray of hope was left for him to dwell upon, and it was folly and madness to be struggling against what appeared so palpably to be our fixed and settled destiny. I remonstrated with him as effectually as the weakness both of my body and my understanding would allow. What I said appeared, for a moment, to have a considerable effect. He made a powerful and sudden effort, half rose up, crawled forward and hoisted the jib, and firmly and loudly cried that he would not give up, that he would live as long as the rest of us.

But, alas, this effort was but the hectic fever of the moment, and he shortly again relapsed into a state of melancholy and despair. This day his reason was attacked, and about nine o'clock in the morning, he became a most miserable spectacle of madness. He spoke incoherently about everything, calling loudly for a napkin and water, and then— lying stupidly and senselessly down in the boat again— closed his hollow eyes, as if in death.

About ten o'clock, we suddenly perceived that he had become speechless. We got him, as well as we were able, upon a board, which was placed on one of the seats of the boat, and after covering him up with some old clothes, we left him to his fate.

He lay in the greatest pain and apparent misery, groaning

piteously until four o'clock in the afternoon, when he died in the most horrid and frightful convulsions I ever witnessed. We kept his corpse all night. In the morning my two companions began, as a matter of course, to make preparations to dispose of it in the sea when, having reflected on the subject all night, I addressed them on the painful subject of keeping the body for food! Our provisions could not possibly last us beyond three days. Within this time it was not in any degree probable that we should find relief from our present sufferings, and, accordingly, hunger would at last drive us to the necessity of casting lots. It was without any objection agreed to, and we set to work as fast as we were able to prepare the body so as to prevent its spoiling. We separated the limbs from the body and cut all the flesh from the bones, after which we opened the body, took out the heart, closed it again—sewing it up as decently as we could—and then committed it to the sea.

We now first commenced to satisfy the immediate cravings of nature from the heart, which we eagerly devoured. We then ate sparingly of a few pieces of the flesh, after which we hung up the remainder, cut in thin strips, about the boat to dry in the sun. We made a fire and roasted some of it to serve us during the next day.

In this manner did we dispose of our fellow sufferer, the painful recollection of which brings to mind, at this moment, some of the most disagreeable and revolting ideas that it is capable of conceiving. We knew not then to whose lot it would fall next either to die or to be shot and eaten like the poor wretch we had just dispatched. Humanity must shudder at the dreadful recital. I have no language to paint the anguish of our souls in this dreadful dilemma.

The next morning, the 10th of February, we found that the flesh had become tainted and had turned a greenish colour. We concluded to make a fire and cook it at once to prevent its becoming so putrid as not to be eatable at all. We, accordingly, did so and, by that means, preserved it for six or seven days longer. Our bread during the time remained untouched. As that would not be liable to spoil, we placed it carefully aside for the last moments of our trial.

About three o'clock this afternoon, February 10th, a strong breeze set in from the northwest, and we made very good progress, considering that we were compelled to steer the boat by management of the sails alone. This wind continued until the 13th, when it changed again ahead.

We contrived to keep soul and body together by sparingly partaking of our flesh, which was cut up in small pieces and eaten with salt water. By the 14th, our bodies became so far recruited as to enable us to make a few attempts at guiding our boat again with the oar. By each taking his turn, we managed to steer it and to make a tolerably good course.

On the 15th our flesh was all consumed. We were driven to the last morsel of bread, consisting of two cakes. Our limbs had, for the last two days, swelled very much and now began to pain us most excessively. We were still, as near as we could judge, three hundred miles from land, with but three days of our allowance on hand. The hope of a continuation of the wind, which came out of the west this morning, was the only comfort and solace that remained to us. So strong had our desires at last become in respect to the wind that a high fever and a longing had set in our veins, which nothing but its continuation could satisfy. Matters with us were now at their height. All hope was cast upon the breeze, and we tremblingly and fearfully awaited its progress and the dreadful development of our destiny.

On the 16th, at night, full of the horrible reflections of our situation and panting with weakness, I lay down to sleep, almost indifferent whether I should ever see the light again. I had not lain long before I dreamt I saw a ship at some distance off from us. I strained every nerve to get to her but could not. I awoke almost overpowered with the frenzy I had caught in my slumbers and stung with the cruelties of a diseased and disappointed imagination.

On the 17th, in the afternoon, a heavy cloud appeared to be setting down in an east by north direction from us, which, in my view, indicated the vicinity of some land. This I took for the island of Más Afuera. I concluded it could be no other; and immediately upon this reflection, the life blood began to flow again briskly in my veins. I told my companions that I was well convinced it was land, and, if so, we should in all probability reach it before two days more.

"The captain hailed us and asked who we were."

My words appeared to comfort my companions much. By repeated assurances of the favourable appearance of things, their spirits acquired even a degree of elasticity that was truly astonishing. The dark features of our distress began now to diminish a little and the countenance, even amid the gloomy bodings of our hard lot, to assume a much fresher hue. We directed our course for the cloud, and our progress that night was extremely good.

The next morning, before daylight, Thomas Nickerson—a boy about fifteen years of age and one of my two companions who had thus far survived with me—lay down after having bailed the boat, drew a piece of canvas over himself, and cried out that he then wished to die immediately. I saw that he had given up, and I attempted to speak a few words of comfort and encouragement to him. I endeavoured to persuade him that it was a great weakness, and even a wickedness, to abandon a reliance upon the Almighty while the least hope and breath of life remained. But he felt unwilling to listen to any of the consolatory suggestions which I made to him, and he insisted—notwithstanding the extreme probability which I stated there was of our gaining the land before the end of two days more—upon lying down and giving himself up to despair.

A fixed look of settled and forsaken despondency came over his face. He lay for some time silent, sullen, and sorrowful. I felt at once certain that the coldness of death was fast gathering upon him. There was a sudden and unaccountable earnestness in his manner that alarmed me and made me fear that I myself might unexpectedly be overtaken by a like weakness or dizziness of nature, which would bereave me at once of both reason and life. But Providence willed it otherwise.

At about seven o'clock this morning, February 18th, while I was lying asleep, my companion who was steering suddenly and loudly called out: *"There's a sail!"*

I know not what was the first movement I made upon hearing such an unexpected cry. The earliest of my recollections is that immediately I stood up and gazed in a state of abstraction and ecstasy upon the blessed vision of a vessel about seven miles off from us. She was standing in the same direction with us, and the only sensation I felt at the moment was that of a violent and unaccountable impulse to fly directly towards her. I do not believe it is possible to form a just conception of the pure, strong feelings and the unmingled emotions of joy and gratitude that took possession of my mind on this occasion. The boy, too, took a sudden and animated start from his despondency and stood up to witness the probable instrument of his salvation.

Our only fear now was that she would not discover us or that we might not be able to intercept her course. However, we immediately put our boat—as well as we were able—in a direction to cut her off and found, to our great joy, that we sailed faster than she did. Upon observing us, she shortened sail and allowed us to come up to her. The captain hailed us and asked who we were.

I told him we were from a wreck, and he cried out immediately for us to come alongside the ship. I made an effort to assist myself along to the side, for the purpose of getting up, but strength failed me altogether, and I found it impossible to move a step further without help.

We must have formed at that moment, in the eyes of the captain and his crew, a most deplorable and affecting picture of suffering and misery. Our cadaverous countenances, sunken eyes, and bones just starting through the skin—with the ragged remnants of clothes stuck about our sunburnt bodies—must have produced an appearance to him affecting and revolting in the highest degree. The sailors commenced to remove us from our boat, and we were taken to the cabin and comfortably provided for in every respect. In a few minutes we were permitted to taste of a little thin food, made from tapioca, and in a few days, with prudent management, we were considerably recruited.

Our rescue vessel proved to be the brig *Indian*, Captain William Crozier of London, to whom we are indebted for every polite, friendly, and attentive disposition towards us that can possibly characterize a man of humanity and feeling. We were taken up in latitude 33° 45' south, longitude 81° 03' west. At twelve o'clock on this same day, we saw the island of Más Afuera, and on the 25th of February, we arrived at Valparaiso in utter distress and poverty. Our wants were promptly relieved there.

Captain Pollard and the lone survivor of his boat's crew were taken up by the American whaleship *Dauphin*, Captain Zimri Coffin of Nantucket. They arrived at Valparaiso on the following 17th of March. They had been taken up in latitude 37° south off the island of St. Mary. The third boat got separated from the captain on the 28th of January and has not been heard of since.

The names of all the survivors are as follows: Captain George Pollard, Junior, Charles Ramsdell, Owen Chase, Benjamin Lawrence, and Thomas Nickerson, all of Nantucket. There died in the captain's boat the following: Brazilla Ray of Nantucket, Owen Coffin of the same place, who was shot, and Samuel Reed, a black.

The captain relates that after being separated from us, as herein before stated, they continued to make what progress they could towards the Juan Fernández Islands as was agreed upon. But contrary winds and the extreme debility of the crew prevailed against their united exertions. He was, like ourselves, equally surprised and concerned at the separation that took place between us, but continued on his course, almost confident of meeting with us again.

On the 14th of January, the whole stock of provisions belonging to the second mate's boat was entirely exhausted. On the 25th, the black man, Lawson Thomas, died and was eaten by his surviving companions. On the 21st, the captain and his crew were in the like dreadful situation with respect to their provisions. On the 23rd, another coloured man, Charles Shorter, died, and his body was shared for food between the crews of both boats. On the 27th, Isaiah Shepherd, a black man, died in the third boat, and on the 28th, another black named Samuel Reed died out of the captain's boat. The bodies of these men constituted their only food while it lasted.

On the 28th of January, owing to the darkness of the night and want of sufficient power to manage their boats, those of the captain and the second mate separated in latitude 35° south, longitude 100° west. On the 1st of February, having consumed their last morsel, the captain and the three other men that remained with him were reduced to the necessity of casting lots. It fell upon Owen Coffin to die. With great fortitude and resignation, he submitted to his fate. They drew lots to see who should shoot him. He placed himself firmly to receive his death and was immediately shot by Charles Ramsdell, whose hard fortune it was to become his executioner.

On the 11th, Brazilla Ray died. The captain and Charles Ramsdell, the only two that were then left, subsisted on the two bodies until the morning of the 23rd of February, when they fell in with the ship *Dauphin*, as before stated, and were snatched from impending destruction.

Every assistance and attentive resource of humanity was bestowed upon them by Captain Coffin, to whom Captain Pollard acknowledged every grateful obligation. Upon making known the fact—that three of our companions had been left at Ducie Island—to the captain of the U.S. frigate *Constellation*, which lay at Valparaiso when we arrived, that officer said he should immediately take measures to have them taken off.

On the 11th of June following, I arrived at Nantucket in the whaleship *Eagle*, Captain William H. Coffin. My family had received the most distressing account of our shipwreck and had given me up for lost. My unexpected appearance was welcomed with the most grateful obligations and acknowledgments to a beneficent Creator, who had guided me through darkness, trouble, and death, once more to the bosom of my country and friends.

The following is a list of the whole crew of the ship, with their arrangements into the three boats upon starting from the wreck.

FIRST WHALEBOAT

Captain George Pollard, Junior	Survived
Obed Hendricks	Put in third boat. Missing
Brazilla Ray	Died
Owen Coffin	Shot
Samuel Reed	Died
Charles Ramsdell	Survived
Seth Weeks	Left on the island

SECOND WHALEBOAT

Owen Chase	Survived
Benjamin Lawrence	Survived
Thomas Nickerson	Survived
Isaac Cole	Died
Richard Peterson	Died
William Wright	Left on the island

THIRD WHALEBOAT

Matthew P. Joy	Died
Thomas Chapple	Left on the island
Joseph West	Missing
Lawson Thomas	Died
Charles Shorter	Died
Isaiah Shepherd	Died
William Bond	Missing

EPILOGUE

——⧓——

Some men die at ebb tide; some at low water;
some at the full of the flood . . .

HERMAN MELVILLE
Moby Dick

News of the three crewmen from the *Essex* who had been left on Ducie Island did not reach Nantucket until after Owen Chase's book was published in the late fall of 1821. As it turned out, these men—William Wright, Seth Weeks, and Thomas Chapple—waited on the island over three months for a passing ship to rescue them. They were picked up finally on April 5, 1821, by the *Surrey,* a British vessel bound for Australia.

On the day of their rescue, according to the story later told by Thomas Chapple, the castaways were combing the island's cliffs and crags for food and water as usual when they were startled by a sound that they thought at first was distant thunder. Turning toward the sea, however, they caught sight of the *Surrey* in the offing, which had fired a gun to make her presence known. After hastening to the shore as rapidly as their weakened conditions would allow, the three seamen

——⧓——

91

saw a boat from the vessel steering toward them. But, unfortunately, the *Surrey* had arrived on the side of the island that was bounded by steep rocks, and her launch could not approach the shore at low tide. In a rash attempt to swim out to his rescuers, Thomas Chapple plunged into the sea, where he almost drowned at the final moment of his long ordeal. William Wright and Seth Weeks more cautiously crawled out onto the rocks where, after a great deal of hard work on the part of the *Surrey*'s crew, they were finally taken aboard the launch.

The *Surrey*'s Captain Raine learned of the plight of the three seamen from the *Essex* when, shortly after rounding Cape Horn, he sailed his ship into the Chilean seaport of Valparaiso. There he was paid three hundred dollars by the U.S. naval officer whom Captain Pollard had entrusted with the rescue of the castaways to pass by Ducie Island on his way across the Pacific. When the *Surrey* reached Ducie Island, however, Captain Raine found no trace of the three seamen. He then sailed northeast in the hope of finding the men from the *Essex* on another island about which he had been told in Valparaiso by Captain Henderson of the whaleship *Hercules* and which lay in that direction. Fortunately for the castaways, the British shipmaster's information turned out to be correct. The island that the men from the *Essex* had reached in their frail whaleboats on December 20, 1820, was not Ducie Island, as they had supposed, but a nameless, mountainous landfall over two hundred miles away.

In the belief that the captain of the *Hercules* had been the island's original discoverer, Captain Raine gave the rocky place the name of Henderson Island, which it has been called ever since. Actually, however, the island had been inhabited before either Captain Henderson or the whalemen from the *Essex* ever came across it. While searching for a shelter, the three castaways, as Thomas Chapple also reported, had discovered eight human skeletons in one of the island's natural caves. These remains were stretched out neatly in a row on the floor of the cave, as if the eight had deliberately decided to lie down and die together. In all probability, as the castaways grimly surmised, the skeletons belonged to shipwrecked seamen—possibly even from the ship *Elizabeth,* whose name had been found earlier carved on the bark of one of the island's trees.

The tin box from the *Essex* that Captain Pollard had nailed to this same tree before leaving the island was taken aboard the *Surrey* and opened by Captain Raine. Of the letters that the former master of the *Essex* had written and sealed inside the box, the content of only one is known. In this letter, the captain's main purpose was to note the essential details of the shipwreck in case none of the crew should remain to tell the tale. The letter ends pathetically:

> *We intend to leave tomorrow, which will be the 26th of December, 1820, for the continent. I shall leave with this a letter for my wife, and whoever finds and have the goodness to forward it, will oblige an unfortunate man, and receive his sincere wishes.*
>
> GEORGE POLLARD, JUNIOR.

The five men from the *Essex* who survived the two-thousand-mile voyage from Henderson Island to the continent of South America were reunited, as Owen Chase has stated, on March 17, 1821. At the time that they were picked up at sea, Captain Pollard and Charles Ramsdell had been shipwrecked a total of ninety-five days while Owen Chase and his surviving companions—Benjamin Lawrence and Thomas Nickerson—had been shipwrecked for ninety days. Since leaving the waterlogged remains of their wrecked ship on November 22, 1820, they sailed their two whaleboats a distance of more than thirty-five hundred miles. As a feat of seamanship, their achievement recalls the remarkable voyage made by William Bligh, the commander of the *Bounty,* after the famous mutiny aboard that ship in April, 1789. Set adrift by the mutineers with eighteen of his men in a twenty-four-foot launch near Tahiti on April 28, Captain Bligh sailed some four thousand miles across the South Pacific to the Indonesian island of Timor, north of Australia, in forty-seven days.

Ironically enough, Pitcairn Island, which had been settled by mutineers from the *Bounty* in 1790, lay about one hundred and fifty miles southwest of Henderson Island. Whether or not Captain Pollard knew of the proximity of Pitcairn is an open question. Probably he did know of the island's existence—the whereabouts of the *Bounty* colony had been discovered by another Nantucket captain in 1808—but was uncertain of its exact location. Moreover, as he believed he was on Ducie Island, he would have considered himself several hundred miles further away from Pitcairn than he actually was. But in any case, Captain Pollard could not afford to gamble. With an inadequate knowledge of the area, compounded by the lack of provisions and the steadily worsening condition of his men, the former master of the *Essex* had no choice at any time but to set his course in those directions where he was certain land existed.

The first of the eight *Essex* survivors to reach their homes were Owen Chase and the three crewmen from the whaleboats, who returned to Nantucket together from Valparaiso on board the whaleship *Eagle* on June 11, 1821. Captain Pollard, who needed more time to regain his strength, remained in the Chilean seaport for another month. The whaler *Two Brothers,* which brought him back to Nantucket on August 5 of the same year, was, as it turned out, to take him away again a few months later on his final whaling voyage. The remaining three survivors—the Henderson Island castaways who were picked up by the *Surrey* and taken to Australia—returned home by way of London. There William Wright and Seth Weeks parted company with the Englishman, Thomas Chapple. The two American seamen finally made their way back to Barnstable, Massachusetts, in October of 1822, nearly a year after Owen Chase's book was published and more than three years after the *Essex* had sailed from Nantucket.

The story has been told that when the *Eagle,* which was known to be carrying Owen Chase and three other seamen from the *Essex,* arrived at the Nantucket Bar, as the outer entrance to the island's harbor was called, a black flag—the signal of death—was hoisted to her masthead. News of this passed quickly around the island, and a large throng descended on the wharf to greet the *Eagle.* When the seamen from the *Essex,* still gaunt from their ordeal, stepped off the ship, a hush fell upon the waiting crowd. Not a word was spoken as the four men walked slowly away from the wharf and up the street to their homes.

The silence that greeted Owen Chase and his companions on their homecoming was more likely due to awe than to any resentment over the men who would never come back, as has sometimes been implied. It is certainly not true that any stigma of death or bad luck—such as the black flag that was

supposed to have been hoisted to the masthead of the *Eagle*—
was ever attached to them. On an island like Nantucket,
where people were hardened to the realities of sea disasters,
the *Essex* survivors never had to account for their actions
in the whaleboats. Though instances of shipwrecked seamen
who were driven to cannibalism on the open seas were fortunately rare, Nantucketers had heard of other such cases in
the past. In 1816, only a few years before the *Essex* disaster,
the crew of a French frigate, the *Mignonette*, had been driven
to the same extreme. Brought ashore at Falmouth, England,
the French seamen were tried for their actions in a court of
law. The story they told, however, aroused such sympathy for
them that they were immediately pardoned and released.

In line with the tradition of their island, the five survivors
from the *Essex* all courageously turned to the sea again for
their livelihoods. Though they were all eventually addressed
as "Captain," according to Nantucket records only two of
them besides Captain Pollard—Owen Chase and Benjamin
Lawrence—actually commanded whaling vessels. The former master of the *Essex* sailed back to the Pacific as the
captain of the *Two Brothers* on November 26, 1821. But he
was dogged by ill luck. Fourteen months later—in March,
1823—while cruising northwest of the Hawaiian Islands, his
ship struck an uncharted coral reef and was totally wrecked.
This time, however, the unfortunate shipmaster was at least
spared the ordeal of a second long open-boat voyage. A few
days after the wreck of the *Two Brothers,* he and his crew
were picked up by another Nantucket whaler, the *Martha,*
and deposited on one of the nearby islands.

While making his way back to Nantucket, Captain Pollard
took passage on board the U.S. brig *Pearl*, which stopped for

repairs at Raiatéa, one of the Society Islands in the southern Pacific. There, on April 16, 1823, the discouraged whaleman encountered two English missionaries who had been sent out from London on an eight-year tour of Asia and the South Sea Islands. These men, Daniel Tyerman and George Bennet, wrote down the captain's story in one of the many journals that they kept to record their experiences. In 1831, their journals were compiled into a book and published.

As filtered through the missionaries, Captain Pollard's brief version of the *Essex* disaster does not tally with Owen Chase's account in many places. This is not surprising, however, in view of the long time lapses between the *Essex* shipwreck, the captain's meeting with the missionaries, and the publication of the latter's journals. Of more importance is the glimpse the narrative gives of Captain Pollard's state of mind. After the loss of his second ship, the former master of the *Essex* was, understandably, a broken and dispirited man. As he finished his account of the shooting of Owen Coffin, he gave way to his emotions.

"But I can tell you no more," he cried out. "My head is on fire at the recollection; I hardly know what I say."

When he had recovered himself, the despondent whaleman turned to the painful subject of his second shipwreck. After reciting the main facts of this disaster, he concluded his recollections, according to the missionaries, in a tone of complete despair.

"Now I am utterly ruined," he said. "No owner will ever trust me with a whaler again, for all will say that I am an unlucky man."

True to his own prophecy, Captain Pollard never returned to the sea. Although he was only thirty-three years old when he came back to Nantucket in April of 1825, he remained on land until his death forty-five years later at the age of seventy-eight. During this long period, he earned his living as one of the island's night watchmen.

Captain Pollard was a serious, unassuming man who had the respect of his fellow islanders throughout his life. After his death on January 7, 1870, the local Nantucket newspaper printed the following comment about him:

> He now leaves a record of a good and worthy man as a legacy to us who remain.

The bad luck that pursued Captain Pollard did not hold for the other two *Essex* survivors who became whaleship captains. After making several voyages to the Pacific from Nantucket as a mate, Benjamin Lawrence traveled to Hudson, New York, where he successively commanded the whalers *Huron* and *Dromo*. When he retired from the sea in 1841, he returned to Nantucket and became a farmer. He died on March 28, 1879, at the age of eighty.

Owen Chase's career as a whaling captain began in 1832 when he was given command of the *Charles Carroll*, one of the few large ships ever built on Nantucket. As the master of this vessel, he made two profitable trips to the Pacific, returning each time with a cargo of over two thousand barrels of sperm whale oil. On his final voyage, however, he complained of pains in his head. These apparently harked back to his suffering at the time of the *Essex* shipwreck, and though he lived on for many years after he retired from the sea in February of 1840, they continued to plague him. In addition, he was haunted toward the end of his life by a fear of starvation, which led him to hoard crackers and other food in the attic of his home. He died on March 7, 1869, at the age of seventy-one.

Owen Chase was the second to die of the five Nantucket survivors of the *Essex* disaster. The first was Charles Ramsdell, the crewman who had been given the unfortunate task of shooting Owen Coffin in Captain Pollard's whaleboat. Ramsdell, who could rarely bring himself to mention the shipwreck, even among his own family, passed away in 1865 at the age of sixty-two.

The fifth survivor and the last to die was Thomas Nickerson, who had been the youngest member of the *Essex*'s crew. An account of an actual interview with Nickerson appeared shortly before his death in 1883 in a New York City newspaper. Although the seventy-eight-year-old mariner was reluctant to discuss his whaleboat ordeal, he did attempt to give his impressions of the whale's attack upon the *Essex*. Apart from claiming that the whale rammed the ship three times, the interview in general agrees with Owen Chase's story.

Reports of whaleboats that had been smashed by the fury of a sperm whale were as much a part of Yankee whaling as the scrimshaw that the whalemen carved from whale's teeth on their long sea voyages. Moreover, cases of ships accidentally colliding with whales and being wrecked were not uncommon. Whales, too, had probably unintentionally rammed many ships. But no whale had ever been known to deliberately attack and sink a vessel before the *Essex*. As a result, the wreck of the Nantucket whaleship became a topic of discussion wherever whalemen gathered, on land as well as at sea, while Owen Chase himself became something of a legend during his own lifetime.

Both the former first mate and his ship were destined to

be remembered in a more enduring way. In 1841, a twenty-one-year-old seaman named Herman Melville, who was to become one of America's greatest novelists, sailed from Fairhaven, Massachusetts, aboard the whaleship *Acushnet*. Some ten months later near the equator in the South Pacific, the *Acushnet* met up with a Nantucket whaler, the *Lima*, and the crew of both "gammed" or visited together. On board the *Lima*, Herman Melville met and talked, as he reported later, with "a fine lad of sixteen or thereabouts" who turned out to be a son of Owen Chase. The two held a lengthy conversation about the *Essex*, and when the gam was over, young William Chase lent the future novelist a copy of his father's book. "The reading of this wondrous story," Melville noted, "upon the landless sea, and close to the very latitude of the shipwreck had a surprising effect on me."

What particularly impressed Herman Melville about Owen Chase's account of the sinking of the *Essex* was the way in which the huge whale, seemingly enraged by the attack upon his herd, had deliberately chosen to hurl himself against the ship. Melville could not forget it. Eight years later, he drew on Owen Chase's story when he wrote the climax of his greatest novel, *Moby Dick*. As the great white whale turns his malicious fury on the whaleship *Pequod*, the scene is in many places a powerful echo of Owen Chase's description of the attack upon the *Essex*.

In addition to its literary greatness, *Moby Dick* is a monument to Yankee whaling—particularly to the seamen of Nantucket like Owen Chase to whom Herman Melville paid a special tribute.

"For the sea is his," he wrote of the Nantucket whaleman. "He owns it, as emperors own their empires."

Nantucket's whaling ships and men had begun to leave their "empire," however, long before *Moby Dick* was published in 1851. After reaching a peak of prosperity in the mid-1830s, the whaling fortunes of the island steadily declined. As sperm whales were driven further and further into the extreme corners of the Pacific, it had become necessary to build and equip larger whaleships to make the longer voyages. These new vessels proved too heavy, however, to pass over the series of sand bars at the outer entrance to the island's harbor. To overcome this handicap, the islanders devised a system of floating pontoons known as "camels," which were designed to buoy the large ships across the hazardous shoals. Effective as these camels proved, they could not restore the island's waning industry. Already far outdistanced by New Bedford, Nantucket whaling suffered two other major setbacks in quick succession. In 1846, a fire destroyed the island's wharves while several years later, in the wake of the California Gold Rush of 1849, over four hundred able-bodied men left to seek their fortunes in the West. By 1857, the year New Bedford reached her peak as a whaling port with a fleet of three hundred and twenty-nine ships, Nantucket had only some fifteen whalers to her credit. Her last whaler, the bark *Oak*, sailed to the Pacific in 1869, the same year that Owen Chase died. Although the *Oak* sent back her cargo of whale oil to the island, the ship herself never returned. Instead, she was sold in Panama in 1872.

New Bedford continued to send her whalers out until the second decade of the twentieth century, but the death knell for the Yankee whaling industry had been sounded as early as 1859, when the first American oil well was drilled near Titusville, Pennsylvania. Just as the sperm whale's oil had given a better light than the right whale's, so oil from the earth now proved superior to whale oil and was also easier and cheaper to obtain. There was still a demand, however, for oil from the right whale for lubrication. It was through this type of whaling in Arctic waters that New Bedford was able to keep her fleet of whaleships active for so long a period. But even this great mainland seaport had to give up eventually. In August of 1925, New Bedford's last whaler, the schooner *John R. Manta,* returned from her final whaling voyage. Unloaded and tied up at the wharf, the lone schooner symbolized the passing of an era. No Yankee whaler would ever again set forth under sail to hunt the great whales in the oceans of the earth.

IOLA HAVERSTICK AND
BETTY SHEPARD

GLOSSARY

The following list includes descriptions of the nautical and whaling terms used by Owen Chase in his story. These words do not necessarily have the same meanings today as they did in 1821, and in some cases the vocabulary is regional.

beam-ends   a ship is on her beam-ends when she falls to one side and is in danger of capsizing

binnacle   the stand containing the ship's compass

brace about   to come about; to change course relative to the wind using the ship's yards

breach   the leap of a whale out of the water; the breach (now spelled breech) of a gun is the part located behind the barrel

bulkhead   a partition below deck that separates space into compartments

cambouse   a furnace equipped with pots on the dock of a whaling ship where a whale's blubber was boiled down to oil

ceiling   the interior wooden planking of a ship

chains   strong iron plates bolted through a ship's sides which help secure the stays, supporting the masthead

clinker built built with overlapping boards

fathom	a unit of measure for the depth at sea, equal to two yards
floor	the supporting timbers which make up the sole of the boat
free	a vessel is free when the water has been pumped out of her
flying jib	a secondary sail set outside the jib on an extended boom; a jib is a triangular sail which extends from the top of the foremast to the large spar at the stem of the ship
gill	a liquid unit equal to one-fourth of a pint
gunwhale	the upper railing of a ship or boat
heave to	a maneuver to slow or stop a ship
hove aback	the past tense of heave aback—a way of stopping or slowing a ship by reducing sail or causing the sails to counteract
knot	one nautical mile per hour
lanyards	rope used to extend the beams that support the masts of a ship
lay off	past tense of lie off—to keep a ship a short distance away from the shore or another ship
lee bow	the sheltered side of the bow
leeward	away from the wind
peppergrass	a type of plant similar to watercress
plank shear	outer edge of a deck

practical navigators	handbooks on navigation
put away	to place a ship in position to sail in a particular direction
quarter	part of a ship's side located between the beam and the stern
rasp	a coarse file with distinct points like teeth
rod	a unit of length equal to sixteen and one-half feet
sheer off	to deviate a ship from its course
shoal	a group of whales, the same as a herd or school of whales
spissy	an archaic word meaning dense or thick
sprit-sails	sails rigged on a pole which extends diagonally from the mast
starting	loosening
stem	the center timber at the bow of a ship
sternpost	the center timber at the stern of a ship
streak	a variation of the word "strake"—a continuous sheet of planking in the hull
waist	portion of the upper deck forward of the mast and the quarter deck
weather	the direction from which the wind blows. The weather side of the ship is the side next to the wind
whetstone	a stone for sharpening tools

working   the ship is working when her joints and
seams begin to separate slowly

yard   a long spar set across a mast to spread and
support a sail